MAKE IT LAST FOREVER

A LOVING MARRIAGE, WORKS

Wayne & Kimberly Colbert

ROYSTON
Publishing

BK Royston Publishing
P. O. Box 4321
Jeffersonville, IN 47131
502-802-5385
http://www.bkroystonpublishing.com
bkroystonpublishing@gmail.com

© Copyright – 2019

All Rights Reserved. No part of this book may be reproduced, stored in a retrieval system, or transmitted by any means without the written permission of the author.

Cover Design: Gad – Elite Covers

ISBN-13: 978-1-946111-73-9

Printed in the United States of America

Dedication and Thanks

We would like to dedicate this book to our wonderful and loving parents who believed in us, our marriage and family; Herbert and Louise Morris and Dr. Herman and Mary Colbert, for without you, there would be no Wayne and Kim. Our marriage has last for over thirty years because of your consistent love, support, guidance and holistic teachings. Thank you for giving us your constant and consistent love, ears, wisdom and solid teachings which will last forever. You will forever be alive in our heart and marriage. To our four beautiful and loving children, Brandi, Damon (*RaLonda*), J'Keeta and Jermaine and numerous grandchildren. Thanks for always encouraging us and believing in us as parents and grandparents. You are the best and we love each of you deeply. To the family of Kingdom Land Baptist Church, thanks for loving us and supporting us in ministry. We will forever praise and thank God for each one of you.

Finally, we are grateful for our extended strong support system God has blessed us with down through the years. Our beautiful and sweet Aunt Mildred Connor-Morris, Aunt Valtonia Courtney, Aunt Barbara Courtney, and our humble Uncle Howard Courtney. We thank you for providing us to with non-bias support, love and encouragement after we made our mistakes. Thanks for not judging us, but continuing to believe in and pray for us. Thank you, Aunt Claudette Colbert-Davis, and Uncle Marvin, for being a listening ear whenever we needed someone to talk to. You always made time for our calls and opened your doors during our unannounced visits. We say thank you to our dear Uncle James and Aunt Catherine Parker, Uncle Eugene Parker and Theresa Goggins; you are gone from our present, but never from our hearts. To our loving Pastor and mentors Dr. Alex and Elect Lady, Gertrude Moses, thank you for being a blessing to our marriage and family. We will forever be indebted to God and grateful for the godly guidance and wise counsel you have given us. Thank you for allowing God to use your marriage as a model to show us what Holy Matrimony looks like in His eyes. Your loving marriage, words of encouragement, guidance and hope for us, always said "With God and Love, Our Marriage Will Last Forever."

Table of Content

Dedication and Thanks	iii
Introduction	vii
Get A Love J.O.N.E.S.	1
Prayer Works	17
Am I Ready to Say "I DO?"	29
Get A Mountaintop Marriage	47
Live in the Spirit of Unity	67
The Pursuit of Unity	77
Eating Healthy Together	83
Do A Pop-Up	113
Honey, I Need Your Support Not Complaints	121

INTRODUCTION

True lovers always work together. If there is a problem for one, it is a problem in the marriage, and it needs to be worked out. However, if it is good for one, it should be good for the two. Many couples desire to have a loving marriage, which lasts forever, and they should. Yet, many lose faith and hope in working to create that loving and lasting marriage they desire. When difficulties arise in their marriage, they refuse or ignore addressing them. Their method is to ignore it and only deal with it in their mind or wish them away. Later down the road, the marriage they began settling for is the one that looks completely opposite of the one they hoped for and dreamed of.

Many husband's feel overwhelmed because they think they haves to be the fixer of all things but lack the tools, resources, and help to accomplish what is needed. The thought of him seeking help makes him think he would be viewed as a weak husband who is unable to provide and protect his wife. The more the issues that are present in their marriage, the stronger the thought becomes in his mind. He knows the struggle in mind is real, but keeps it right there, in his mind. Therefore, he fails to seek the help he needs to protect and provide for his spouse.

The wife is dealing with her own issues. She thinks she cannot go another day on overload. She converses with her best friend, herself. She gets the best of both worlds. She gets to ask the questions and answer them. "How can I do all of this? I am one person. How can I continue doing all this by myself? I need help." Therefore, she gives up having hope for achieving the loving marriage she dreamed and prayed for. In her self-evaluation she knows she lacks the strength to continue as the Superwoman she was before their marriage. She tells herself this is what he fell in love with. She still thinks she must continue doing everything by herself, because if she doesn't, he will leave.

Unhealthy thoughts like this, gives birth to things that has the potential of aborting what could be a loving marriage. Stinking thinking will mess you up and others up. This type of thinking can keep her from sharing her thoughts with her husband and from seeing how she was been blessed with help. If she would release or share her thought with and feelings with her Superman, she will discover that she has more than enough help to get the job done.

We believe many marriages can be saved when husband and wife realize God has joined them together to be a super team, which constantly work full-time together as one.

This book teaches couples they need not wait for a problem to arise or to conquer them alone. It provides guidance that will eliminate things from happening in advance. It is an aid to guide couples toward addressing those unaddressed dormant issues in their marriage through conversations. Addressing matters early on can prevent those potential issues from being a huge problem later. This book coaches couples on how to conquer problems when they are identified. We often say in our marriage, "If either of us has a problem, it's unwelcomed in our marriage, then we conquer it together."

This self-help workbook has blessed many couples to become a team and can lead many more toward working as one to overcome their marital challenges together, before these challenges (problems or issues) become a weapon of marital destruction. No one person can solve a problem in a marriage or save a marriage. It takes two to get married and it takes two to make a marriage work and it requires the same two working together to save a faltering or crumbling marriage. If it is to last forever, the two must be willing to put in the work.

Often couples spend money on things their spouse already possesses. Couples must learn to tap into the resource, which lies right next to them, called "Spouse".

Trusting your other half (spouse is a benefit to you. When a husband or wife has trust in one another, they will not hesitate to invest their wisdom and knowledge into them.

This easy to read workbook does not require couples to spend lots of time reading together, rather it requires much time communicating and working as one. This means it requires them setting time aside to work as one for their union. This book provides guidance for approaching their needs by asking provoking questions at the end of each chapter. For couples to be successful in accomplishing their goal, the two must agree to work together as one. For how can two stay married together and make it last forever unless they agree. "Can two walk together, unless they agree?" [Amos 3:3 NKJV]

MAKE IT LAST FOREVER

A LOVING MARRIAGE, WORKS

GET A LOVE J.O.N.E.S.

John 21:15-17 [NKJV]

15 So when they had eaten breakfast, Jesus said to Simon Peter,
"Simon, son of Jonah, do you love Me more than these?"
He said to Him, "Yes, Lord; You know that I love You."
He said to him, "Feed My lambs."
16 He said to him again a second time, "Simon, son of Jonah, do you love Me?"
He said to Him, "Yes, Lord; You know that I love You."
He said to him, "Tend My sheep."
17 He said to him the third time, "Simon, son of Jonah, do you love Me?" Peter was grieved because He said to him the third time, "Do you love Me?"
And he said to Him, "Lord, You know all things; You know that I love You."
Jesus said to him, "Feed My sheep."

Have you ever had a Love Jones for someone and he or she didn't love you back? Many people today are frustrated because they seem to give their all to others but never get back anything close to what they have given. Sometimes it involves married couples. At other times, it involves people dating. This feeling of frustration sometimes involves relationships between parents and children or among siblings. Yes, it may even involve the person you are sitting right next to. It is a part of human nature to want our acts of love appreciated and returned. When our love is not returned, we are sometimes thrown for a loop and suffer.

There are four types of love and all but one of them requires love to love back to exist. Eros, or romantic love is the love that generally exists in romance. It operates when both partners love back. Philia, or brotherly love also works best when returned. Acts of brotherly love, compassion and friendship thrive when returned by the recipient. Storge, or the love between family members such as father to son, mother and daughter is also dependent, to a great extent, upon reciprocity. When a mother loves a child, this love grows best when the mother is loved back. The ideal love however is Agape. It is the love that God has for everyone. It does not require the recipient to love back. It exists and even grows stronger even if it is not returned.

Most of us spend our lives trying to achieve this agape love. Some parents have achieved it for their children. They love, even though they are not being loved back. Some people work to help their fellowman and continue to show them love even though those same people seldom love them back or may do something terrible to hurt them. There are those who are in a relationship experiencing that perfected agape love. They have moved to a level in their relationship whereby they have perfected the ability to love a spouse even though they are not getting that same love reciprocated. Many people have spent years running around investing in a relationship that continues to go in circles. One if not both may become frustrated with themselves feeling as though they have been involved in a one-sided love affair.

I recall my father telling me about a man who filed for a divorce against his wife. He shared how the husband had one day stormed out the house, saying to his wife "I will never come back again to you." Two weeks later, he wrote his ex-wife a very beautiful love letter which said, "Darling, I am so angry with myself. I am sorry, that I lost my temper at the wrong time. I now know you only tried to love me, but I wouldn't love you back. You gave me your heart and I broke it. You gave me your affections and I trampled them. You gave me your love and I squandered it. I now realize what a fool I have been. I can't sleep thinking about you. Being away from you is breaking my heart. I want to love you, like you have loved me and enjoy our life together as partners. Will you forgive me? with all my love, yours truly, your husband. P.S. Congratulations on winning the million-dollar lottery last week!

I tell you there is nothing like a million dollars to jolt us into reality!

Marriage requires two individuals loving their spouse as God loves. A marital goal should always be to perfect or mature in perfect love. Perfect love will drive out all those things and people which seek to hinder, damage or separate love for one another. God's love for us is the perfect example. I long for a relationship that has a love like God. God loved us when we couldn't love Him back, even in our stubbornness, rebelliousness, and insecurities, He loved us anyway. When we messed up, He forgave us before we asked. This is the love we should strive to achieve, whether single or married. Many if not most marriages have not achieved this level of love. This love doesn't happen overnight and neither will it happen immediately after you say "I Do." To achieve perfect love, it must be sought daily and worked out to protect and maintain it.

Brothers and sisters, Love has always been part of God's plan for our lives. We find in Ecclesiastes 3:8 "There is a time to love." Love is greater than faith or hope (I Cor.13:13). The greatest subject in the Bible is love. It's a subject that affects all people. Even the worst sinner desires to be loved. Love has life-changing power…

Power to change your attitude.

Power to change your marriage.

Power to change our family.

Power to change your children.

Power to change your church.

Power to change the roughest neighborhoods and communities.

Power to change our broken school system.

Power to change our hateful politicians

Power to change your future.

LOVE has the power to make you DO RIGHT, when you want to do wrong.

LOVE has the power to bring you home at night.

LOVE has the Power to change YOU.

Have you ever experienced the power of love before and after the marital altar? I know there are those who want to experience this love changing power. To do so, one must learn how to first RESPECT the power of love.

When we consider God's love for us John 3:16 "For God so loved the world that He gave His only begotten Son, that whosoever believes in Him shall not perish, but have everlasting life." In 1st John 4:10 it says, "Not that we love God, but He loves us and sent His Son." Can I share some good news with you? God loves you and He believes in your marriage! The Bible is God's love letter to us all. I remember a love song, by the group "Brighter Side of Darkness" explaining what a Love Jones is…

I tell you if we say we Love God, then today we must have a LOVE JONES for your own spouse and determined to make your marriage last forever. The Brighter Day was singing about that "Cupid Love/Eros Love." However, the Bible, God's Love Letter, gives a whole different meaning of a Love Jones.

Having a Love J.O.N.E.S. for one another, requires us to love God first. (Matthew 22:37 Jesus declares "Love the Lord God with all your heart, soul and mind.") Who is first in your life? In the fore mentioned scripture Jesus is saying a person is to love God first and with their total being, holding nothing back or putting no one before Him. When a person loves God first, they will see the need to love themselves as Christ loves them. It is then they can love and treat others with that same love.

Kim and I are often asked "How did ya'll make it, this long?" We smile and tell them we are still together because we love each other according to the Word of God. We love God first and each other next. We keep God at the top of our priority list. Having God as the head of our lives and Christ in the center, is the fuel we use to empowered our love. Without God there would be no adhesive strong enough to keep our marriage together as one loving couple. Does that mean we will have no problems? No! We have problems like all other couples. We are two different individuals with two different needs and views. These things can be problematic within itself. Yet, we have learned when things go wrong in our marriage to depend on God and allow His Holy Power to be our compass leading us to make right the wrongs. Therefore, we ask ourselves "What Would God Do?" When we consider God, it helps us to do what is right toward each other and we are always pleased with the outcome.

In the earlier scriptures Jesus and His disciples had just eaten breakfast, when Jesus asked Peter the question, "Simon, son of Jonah, do you love Me more than these?"

Wayne and I have developed a Love J.O.N.E.S. for one another. It did not happen overnight, but it happened. This love what we have is something we must work hard on to keep. Let me go ahead and breakdown what a LOVE J.O.N.E.S. is. God is love. [I John 4:16]. When you have the love of God in you, His love will move in and through you.

Love—Jesus (John 21:15, Do you love Me more these; Matt.10:37, He who loves father or mother more than Me is not worthy of Me. And he who loves son or daughter more than Me is not worthy of Me. Do you love the one, who laid His life down for you? Do you love the One who sacrificed heaven to save a sinner like you and I… Jesus loves us so much, that he came down right in our stinky stuff just to redeem us.

You can't love God without loving falling in Love with Jesus. Jesus said no man comes to the Father, but by Me. Jesus is the doorway to God.

When you fall in love with JESUS, you can't help but to love Others (Phil. 2:4 [NKJC] "Let each of you look out not only for his own interests, but also for the interests of others.") When you love Jesus and others, it will give you away. Love is an action word. It's good to hear the words from our spouse "I love you." Yet, it is better when one can see and feel the love. L.O.V.E. will cause you to: Look for excuses to be the first to forgive and forget. Optimize each other's worth. Vocalize affirmation through daily compliments. Express unlimited grace by making mistakes on the side of love and not judgment.

Falling in Love with Jesus is so powerful. It will cause you to FEED others, TEND to others, FEED them some more. This includes our spouse. When our spouse is being fed at home, they will not leave the house with an appetite for something they don't need. The enemy is seeking for opportunities to come in and wreck your home. My husband and I have made it a habit to compliment one another before we leave the house. Therefore, when the enemy gives us one, we won't lose our mind, due to starvation of a compliment.

Having a Love Jones is so powerful, it will spill over into your marriage. When love is present and active in the marriage, it is hard for one to withhold love from the other one. Love will give you hope during hardships and difficult circumstances. Love for your spouse will cause you to declare in the name of Jesus, "This love for my spouse means it will endure forever and I won't give up on our love." We are good at speaking life over many things and people, yet we need to learn to speak life over and into our marriage. I spoke life in our marriage before we took our vows and today, we are stilling speak life over every dead thing and into one another. Speak life in the face of opposition and watch what God does on your behalf. Matt.15:30, "Then great multitudes came to Him, having with them the lame, blind, mute, maimed, and many others; and they laid them down at Jesus' feet, and He healed them." Matt.27:42, "He (Jesus) saved others..." The Love of God and Jesus requires you to love who they love. Love will cause you to love those who don't look like you, even your spouse. During times when you and your spouse are not looking and working as one, God's love will say, "I still love you." Love is not based on what they do for the moment, but based on who they are.

When you love one another with the love God loves, you can't help but to love them "AS IS." Our love for one another should not be predicated on their flawlessness, but despite their flaws. When you have a Love Jones, your love won't discriminate, be racist, and you won't be prejudice with your love.

Now, that you love Jesus and Others, you must love your Neighbors (Mark 12:33, And to love Him (the Lord God) with all the heart, with all the understanding, with all the soul, and with all the strength, and to love one's neighbor as oneself, is more than all the whole burnt offerings and sacrifices. Rom. 13:10 "Love does no harm to a neighbor; therefore, love is the fulfillment of the law." If we had more people who loved their neighbors, the crime rate would decrease and marriages will last. We have too many couples were one spouse doesn't love a neighbor for various strange reasons, while the other one does. This lopsided love can bring a strain on a marriage. If one spouse is upset, dislike or resent a person, is it fair for their spouse to feel the same? "No." When these feelings are in the heart of one, they are in the marriage. Loving your neighbors doesn't mean you have to hang out with them, it means you will treat them with respect and the love of God.

I must admit that you see it a lot in women. Love will cause you to believe the best in your spouse and others. Some spouses believe their spouse should have no conversation or business with the opposite sex after they get married. This thinking is lacking love. Where there is no love there is no trust. Where there is no trust, love is absent. Love is about trust. More fellowships will take place in our families, when we love our neighbor. This love will lead to more unity in ministry and less jealousy, competition, and insecurities, knowing we all are working for the same Kingdom, who are all called by the same Spirit. Having One Lord, One Faith and One Baptist. It's sad to say, but there are people who live in the same house, attending the same church and working in the same workplace, yet, they can't stand one another or their neighbor. "How can you say you love God who you never seen and can't stand your brothers and sisters who you see every day. You are lie and the truth is not in you." I John 4:20] The brotherly love we have for one another should spill over to our neighbors.

WHEN WE LOVE OUR NEIGHBORS.

When you have a LOVE JONES, you will love your Enemies (Matt.5:44, But I say to you, love your enemies, bless those who curse you, do good to those who hate you, and pray for those who spitefully use you and persecute you.

Stop trying to get even with those who hurl insults and attacks against your marriage. All accusation that comes about your spouse should not be believed. When you allow what others say and do to get to you and in you, it provides a way for the enemy to enter your marriage.

Remember, anything you allow to comes in you, come into the marriage and can affect it. If it is not good, leave it alone. God said vengeance is mines. I will repay. Your enemy will not always seek to destroy you, but the one you love. Satan knows he has no chance in destroying God, therefore, he seeks to destroy those whom God loves. You have nothing to prove to others regarding your love for your spouse and you don't have to defend a lie. The only one you have to prove something to regarding your marriage is to God and your spouse. For years Wayne and I have told young couples, "If we don't see it with my own eyes, I will not believe it and we will not believe anything derogatory about one another."

I have had family members and close so call friends trying to tell me something about my husband and vice versa, yet we believe the best about each other; better yet, we trust and love each other so much, to believe anything that's not of God. We can still love those individuals, regardless of their deeds and words were spoken. They have only informed us they do not support our marriage. Therefore, they will do any and everything to destroy it.

Many marriages have crumbed due to a lie. It happens a lot on Social Media. Love will cause you to bless those whom you know don't care anything about you. Do good to those who seek to harm you. REMEMBER, we too were once an enemy, but Jesus loved us, while we were His enemies. God did not start loving us when we starting attending a local church. He loved us before we were a twinkling in our dads....

Finally, Brother and Sister, when you have a LOVE JONES, you will love your Self (Matt.19:19, You shall love your neighbor as yourself. Until you learn to love yourself, you are incapable of loving your spouse and others as yourself. When you love yourself, you will not cut yourself down, belittle yourself, downgrade yourself, LOVE will cause you to encourage yourself when others fail to encourage. When you do these things toward your spouse, you are doing them unto yourself. Loving yourself will cause you to believe what God says about you and your spouse.

When you have a Love Jones for Jesus, there will be valuable signs toward the one you love. A Love Jones for Jesus will provoke you to:

Lift up your spouse bowed down head

Love your spouse when they are oppressed and depressed.

Seek ways to mend your spouse's broken heart or spirit.

Love will rejoice and have hope for one another's success.

Love will cause you to pull your spouse away from what is pulling them down.

Love will cause you to put your spouse's needs first. Love is selfless.

When everything else FAILS, LOVE will LIFT you UP as you LIFT your spouse up.

This love is visible before marriage and gets better and stronger as you work on it, after you say, "I Do."

A MARITAL WORKOUT!

(This workout section may start with one spouse, but should always conclude with both spouses doing the workout.)

Is God first in your life?

_____

Is God first in your spouse's life?

_____

How will putting God first improve your relationship with your spouse?

_____

In what areas of your marriage is God not first?

_____

Why?

_____

Date of acknowledgement.

_____

I have set a goal date to correct what I need to correct.

_____

Does my spouse put God first?

_____

I have set a date to discuss this issue with spouse.

_____

My spouse and I have set a date to start working on this particular area together.

_____

How can your spouse improve in this particular area?

_____

More examples?

_____

What do you suggest your spouse do to improve in this particular area?

_____

Why?

_____

Date of acknowledgement.

_____

Should we seek outside guidance? If so, when, who where?

_____

On today, my spouse and I accomplished this goal together.

_____

PRAYER WORKS

Luke 18:1 says, "Men should always pray and never give up."

Prior to getting married, I recall hearing my pastor giving us some statistics. He said "51 percent of first marriages end in divorce, and 79 percent of second marriages end in divorce, while less than 2 percent of couples who pray together daily end their marriages." Hearing these numbers stuck with us. I recall that night when I prayed, "Lord, please let us be included in the 2 percent." I also recall hearing Kim, chuckling, as she heard my request. Later, we talked about it. Then the one thing she laughed at, became what she prayed for, even to this day. To this day, together we choose to be part of the 2 percent. For over thirty years Kim and I have learned to use prayer as a weapon for our marriage. Why is prayer needed in your marriage? Prayer is a powerful tool God has given us. It invites Him in both persons and is fitting for every situation. Prayer will allow you to talk to God about what you are laughing at in your marriage. Prayer has the power to change you, your prospective of God and the outcome of your marriage.

We heard it said, "The family that prays together stays together." In Luke 18:1 it says "Men should always pray and never give up." In James 5:16 ESV it says "Therefore, confess your sins to one another and pray for one another, that you may be healed. The prayers of a righteous person have great power as it is working." The two scriptures are saying it is okay for couples to prays together and for one another.

I love to see and hear about couples who apply these scriptures to their marriage. Often, people will confess their problems to others, but not the person who they see, eat, and sleep with daily. These two scriptures are very powerful to a marriage. It allows them to admit they have imperfection in their lives. Not so the person can judge them, but so they can receive help. I have always loved praying to God about our marriage and family. Yet, it came a time when it bothered me when I thought about how my husband and I would pray, but not together. We were failing to pray with each other. One day as we were studying the Word of God, our devotion was on these two scriptures. Since that day we have been applying the Word of God. We are not ashamed to confess our sins to one another and pray to our marriage.

Today, I can truly say, there is nothing we can't discuss with each other, even if we know it may hurt or disappoint them. We pray God's strength to help us get over it quick, to avoid that sin spelling over into other areas of our lives or morphing into something else. Praying about situations allows us to admit and agree together that we both need God to guide us through the process, so, his healing and strength may become stronger in our marriage. I challenge you to confess your sins to your spouse. It is not that you are making them God, confessing to one another allows you to close the door on the enemy's weapon called "secrets." Wayne and I have vowed to each other that we would keep no secrets from one another. Often, when a person knows or think they have gotten away with doing something wrong, they will commit that sin again or when the spouse discovers or learns of the secret it is far out of control. It is easier for a person to receive the truth about their spouse from their spouse, than hearing it come from an outside source.

    I recall trying to handle things on my own. Therefore, I kept a deep secret from Wayne regarding our finances. The secret I kept to myself landed us into senseless credit card debt totaling over $35,000. We should be able to communicate with our spouse and do it when sin enters our mind. Your spouse must have your permission to confess to you. They need you to make them feel welcomed prior to them bringing you their problem. I have spoken with many wives who tell me, "My husband says don't bring him anything negative. He doesn't have time for it." Yet, many husbands have shared, "I don't share anything with my wife, because she doesn't know how to handle it or she will go off. I will never live it down." In marriage, we must learn to incline an ear and position our heart and mind to hear not just the good news regarding our spouse, but receive the bad they must share. This gives husbands and wives the opportunity to work together through their struggle. During this time two becomes work by supporting one's weakness. I am glad to say, "With the help of my loving husband, my debt struggle is over."

I challenge you not to be afraid or too proud to pray for and with your spouse regarding their particular needs. Ask your spouse, "What can I pray for? How can I help you?" Don't just pray for what you think they need praying for, ask them and let them be specific. Now, when they tell you what to pray for, don't judge them or make them regret sharing their important matter with you.

We are grateful that prayer is working in our marriage. It is good that Kim and I can talk about what's happening in our marriage. Yet, it is always better when we talk to God about it. God has never failed to make all things better. Before Kim and I said "I Do" we vowed to talk first to God and then to each other. Listed below are some ways our marriage has survived over thirty years and benefitted from prayer:

1. Prayer will humble you. We need to constantly be humbled before God and our spouse. Growing up, I can recall seeing the Deacon's open up devotion with a song and then they would kneel down to pray. I remember seeing the preacher kneeling down to pray, once they mount the pulpit. These acts were expressions of humility. Having humility before God and our spouse will keeps you opened to receive what is needed for your marriage. Having a humbled spirit is an act of worship before God. Humility is quiet, while arrogance is loud. When we go to God on behalf of our spouse, a humble spirit will remind one that we all have sinned and come short of God's Glory. When I pray for Kim's sins, I also include my sins to God. A quite spirit before God will keep us in position to hear from Him, while an arrogance spirit will prevent us from hearing from God and our spouse. Arrogance will cause your voice to become louder than God's. Humility allows us to constantly show our reverence to God and each other. Saying you are humble and showing it is totaling different and both will produce different outcomes.

2. Prayer will break the cycle. Talking to God will cause you to stop hurting yourself (each other). When you

are marriage, you are two who are joined together as one. When you hurt your spouse, you hurt yourself. No one like self-inflicted wounds. When you nurse and rehearse your pain, you are going in circles. When you keep regurgitating how they hurt you, you are going in circles. When you remind them reminisce on the pain and what caused it, you are going to circles. When you pray to God, you give it all to Him. Therefore, when the thought comes to mind, you know not to dwell on it, but to rejoice in the fact that God has delivered you from it. When you talk to God about the pain your spouse caused you, God will guide you into a praise to remind you of how you made it through what the evil one tried to use to destroy you. Prayer will teach you how to put a praise on those things which was meant to destroy you.

Again, when you are humbled in your prayer position, your heart opens to understanding your spouse, rather growing in accusation of them.

3. Prayer will remove it all. Call it out by name. Whatever it is that is hurting you and causing you pain, call it out by name. Just as you call God by His name, your spouse by their name and your neighbor who ask you to pray for them by name, you must call out what is tormenting you by name. When you call people and things by name, you let God knows you are intentional and serious about your

request. When we praise God, we attach a name to that praise. It shall be the same when we are making our request to God, we must put a name on it. Naming your request leads to the road of forgiveness and healing. Whether it is forgiving your spouse of self, it will bring healing in the marriage and pain free. You can place a name to it and call it out by name, because your prayers are for God's ears only, not your spouse or neighbors and He won't tell a soul and remove it all.

4. Prayer brings unity. When we walk together holding hands, it reveals our agreement to walk together. Praying with your spouse reveals your spiritual unity that comes through God's Word and Spirit. When a couple have physical unity and spiritual unity is becomes the glue that bind them together, whereby they are not easily broken.

5. Prayer will birth a thankful heart. When you talk to God about your spouse, He will lead you to thanking Him for your spouse. I don't care how upset you may be with your spouse when you begin talking to God, love will change your conversation to appreciation for them. You will began thanking God for blessing you with the spouse you have. The spouse God has joined you with is fitting just for you. They are not perfect, yet they are perfect for you. Prayer will remind you that you and your spouse are two perfectly,

imperfect people in need of God's guidance for loving one another. When you show God, you appreciate and trust Him; He will show you how to appreciate and love your spouse. When you take your prayer list to God regarding your spouse problems, remember to list how they are a blessing to you. Thank God for blessing you with your spouse. Then love them with their flaws and all.

    6. Prayer is a Change Agent. It invites God into the person and their situation. When you humbled your heart toward God, you will become open to change and growth. Communicating to God your marriage or spouse daily will empower you and renewed a willingness for you to work together toward staying together.

    7. Prayer is not self-centered. There are times when you need to speak to God about yourself, but not all the time. Remember, it's not always about you, at least not when you are praying specially for your spouse. When God reveals something to you about your spouse that is a sign revealing what you should pray for. Regardless, if it is good or bad, talk to God about it. Praying for your spouse causes you to speak to God first about the situation. Therefore, you would know how to approach your spouse. Prayer will guide your words and actions, because you have aligned your purpose

with God's promises and plans, He has purposed for your marriage.

8. Prayer keeps you hopeful. I know someone once said, "Never, say never." Well, prayer says "Never give up on hope." When your hearts are in unity as one with God's good and perfect will, then your prayers will always be answered, even He doesn't grant you the things you prayed for. Remember, when praying to God, He is not bound by our time. He may grant your request later down the road and not immediately after you end the prayer with "Amen." Stay hopeful with your request by waiting on Him to answer. Then accept His answer.

A MARITAL WORKOUT!

(This workout section may start with one spouse, but should always conclude both spouses doing the workout.)

Should you improve on confessing your sin(s) to your spouse?

_____

Why? _____

Should you improve praying more with your spouse?

_____

Why? _____

I have acknowledged on this day

_____

that confessing my sin(s) to my husband and my prayer life with my spouse needs to improve.

I have set a date to communicate my goal of confessing to them and praying with my spouse to my spouse.

_____

How can your spouse help you improve in this area?

_____

Why?

_____

I have set a date for me to discuss this with my spouse on

_____

My spouse and I agree to start praying together on

_____

AM I READY TO SAY "I DO?"

Growing up I recall the first wedding I attended was my cousin named Ginger. As she walked down the aisle to her husband, Paul, I remember she looked like a beautiful African American Doll. On that day, I couldn't wait until I was old enough to get married, so I could dress up wearing a long white gown, with a train that dragged for miles. I envisioned having a beautiful veil lifted up by my husband, while standing in the presence of a massive audience.

I was thinking like most people. When they think of marriage, their minds automatically go to the wedding, not realizing they have to prepare themselves for the life after the walk down and say "I Do." It is after the "I Do" when the two becomes one.

Here are a few questions a person one should ask themselves before becoming married.

- Am I Ready For Marriage?
- Am I ready to live a selfless life?
- Do I really want to spend my life with one person?
- Am I ready to be accountable to and for another life?
- Do I have good credit?

- Am I ready to settle down at this stage in my life?
- Do I really want to be committed to one person for the rest of my life?
- Do I love them and their imperfection?
- Can I support their dreams, careers, and educational goals?
- Is this the right time to include a spouse in my life, when all my time is preserved for achieving my education, dreams and career?
- Am I ready for a family?
- Will I marry someone who already have children?
- Am I willing to be a parent to their child(ren)?
- Can I handle him dealing with the parent of their children?
- Do I love them?
- Etc.

Marriage is more than just a beautiful gown, dance, and lovely celebration. Marriage is a vow that two people make saying they are surrendering living their life alone for a life committed to living with another person, for better or for worse. Most times people focus on the better, because initially each person works hard at doing better and obtaining better things. However, they fail to understand that life is sometimes like the labor market. It will turn a turn with or without one's permission. Therefore, that turn will bring its own problems, issues, struggles, hard aches, and pain. Marriage requires God's Agape Love. A love that will keep loving when things goes wrong, and the resources is little to none. It is easy to love a person when they have everything going for them and when they are in top shape. Yet, many seem to have taken a vow that says, "For better, but forget the worse."

Can you adjust with the seasons?

In most marriages sometimes roles change for a season. The question is how long is a season? I don't know. The season depends on the persons and their circumstances. Your husband may start being a great financial provider for the family. Your family may become use to living on two incomes. However, life sometimes throws us a fast ball we aren't ready for, nothing in life is a one hundred percent guarantee. So, can you handle the seasons as they change and adjust? Now sometimes unexpected circumstances enter in the marriage, which may require you to take on a different role. Can you handle "role play" if life requires you to play the role of being the financial provider for a while. How long is a while? I don't know. It depends on the circumstance.

I recall one time when the season changed in our marriage for a season. Wayne took ill and had major surgery. While he was off work, he exhausted all his salary. We were now entering into a season of receiving one major check when we were accustomed to receiving two. I was working and getting paid; however, it was not enough to cover our cost of living. We had to dip deep into our savings accounts and our rainy-day funds just to pay our monthly bills. During this season, those funds soon became low and eventually depleted. As we both looked at this season together, we didn't like it. Yet, we both understood that life happens. We did not have time to sit around complaining about what he could not do and how much I now had to do. We refused to allow our minds to take a terrible trip down memory lane, reminiscing about how he used to do this or how we use to have that. A journey at this point in your life, can cause one to become bitter about not having what they once had. The love for my husband, children and marriage empowered me to step up and do all I could to help cover my King, without making him feel as though he was less than a King or not a good provider.

Lord knows those thoughts are definitely not true. Wayne came to me to discuss our situation. I fell in love with him even more. It takes a strong man to come to his wife to discuss his need for her help. He didn't allow pride to steer him and I didn't allow self-centeredness to kick in. We worked hard together during this season. I saw it as me being the player and Wayne as my coach. Coach Wayne showed me where we would adjust with our finances and I showed him, how I could run that play, by adjusting with our lifestyle. We both supported each other's new role during this temporal season. Guess what? We won throughout this season. When this phase happens in a marriage, the Coach and Player must learn to work together. Often, I hear women being hard on their husband, when hard times come. This season is when you must remind yourself of who you married.

When you know you have a great provider, don't let ugly thoughts tell you otherwise. The way we had to adjust worked for the good of Wayne and I, which benefitted the entire family. No one was stressed, because God gave us grace to dress our marriage according to the season. We remembered, what we were experiencing was temporal season. Many people are accustomed to the four seasons. Yet, few embrace the temporal season when it comes.

Therefore, their love and marriage dies during this season. Knowing there is a temporal season in life will remind you that what you are experiencing will come to an end.

Today, when unexpected circumstances come up in our marriage Wayne and I have addressed them accordingly and view them as temporary. It doesn't mean we love the season. It means we make adjustments. A temporary season can affect any part of your marriage, not just your finances. Wayne doesn't like the summer because he doesn't like being hot. I don't like the winter because I hate being cold. Yet, when these seasons come, we make adjustments. We have learned to go through life's seasons together, while making sure we both survive the season.

Our lives are not viewed through a crystal ball. Therefore, we don't know what the future has to offers. We do know that life has all types of seasons. These seasons sometimes take a turn for the better and sometimes it's for the worse. Regardless of the season, when love is the center of the marriage, it will become the protector during any inclement season.

Can you see yourself doing it all?

Are you strong enough to get up early in the morning to go to work, while leaving him home? Then coming home having to cook, help the children with their homework, doing laundry, transporting your husband to his doctor's appointments, being your husband's private nurse and still be his private dancer. Are you willing to step up and do it all if circumstances or situation changes during the course your marriage? Can you put your spouse first, even if it means putting your education and professional career on pause for a moment? Notice, I said pause and not halt. Remember, a temporal season may come, which may require you to do so.

Can you balance Family, Ministry and Career?

Does your career or ministry allow you time for a marriage? Many Christians have been heavily involved in ministry and consumed with their career before getting married. Yet, soon afterwards major problems arise because one feels they are being neglected and is secondary to their spouse's ministry and career.

If you are not willing to put your spouse before your career and ministry you may not be ready for marriage at this particular time. Every spouse needs to fill their first priority over everything. When one feels they are not first, they will see you like a cheating spouse with another man or woman. If your spouse is feeling secondary to your ministry and career, it is your responsibility to help your spouse to level up. You must make them feel needed and as valuable as your ministry and career. There is nothing wrong with having a successful ministry and career. However, you must include your spouse in it and remember far most, your marriage should be your first ministry and make it a career to work at "Making It Last Forever."

You working long hours may have been okay before the marriage, but after the marriage your spouse is expecting a change. Therefore, it is very vital to discuss these things before saying "I Do." Your time committed to your career or ministry may not have room for a relationship at this point in your life. Example: Everyone cannot be married to a person who serves in the United States Armed Forces. These men and women may be drafted, relocated, required to travel without family. People with an issue with these things may need to avoid marrying such a person, especially if they are not willing to support their career. Yet, are those who can handle long distance relationship and remain faithful while the other one is away. Their relationship may be developed and become stronger through their conversing with one another over the telephone, until they are united back together. Does this sound like you?

Are the Wounds Open or Closed?

Are you still dealing with the hurt and pain from a previous relationship? Someone once said "Hurt people, hurt people." If you are still dealing with a hurt from a past relationship, don't get a rebound. It's not fair to you and it's definitely not fair to that person. Until your wounds are healed from that thing that harmed you, you will be incapable of loving another person the way they deserve to be loved, you are not ready for anyone in your life.

A wounded heart will only see their wounds and the things which caused them. If you are having numerous thoughts and conversations daily about what happened to you in your past relationship, you are not healed. If you are always nursing and rehearsing your hurt and pains, you are not ready for a relationship. No woman or man wants to hear constantly how you have been hurt from that previous relationship. Yes, they will empathize with you, but when they constantly hear you repeating repeatedly what happened to you, they may begin to feel they have to compete with the last person, not knowing how you will judge them. The relationship will become dictated and controlled by your past, without allowing the new person to prove their love for you. Open wounds will also keep you closed, whereby you can receive the true love you desire and have prayed for.

I recommend before starting a new relationship with another person that you first work on your open wound. This may require you to go to a professional doctor, counselor, therapist, or spiritual counselor like your pastor to get the help you need.

Check Your Love Gauge:

In I Corinthians 13, The Apostle Paul educated the church regarding what love is and how love behaves toward others. Love will cause one to treat people better than they are treated. Love don't seek to get even for a wrong done to them. God ordained marriage to be a union of love. Therefore, marriage is about two people committing to live a life of love. Love must be present before the marriage. Any offense in these areas is a strong recipe for problems in the marriage that could lead to a divorce.

Ask yourself these questions to see if you do these things often. Remember, it is okay to be honest with you. Only when you are honest can you know what you need to get help with.

- Am I impatient?

- Am I rude?
- Am I envious of other?
- Am I puffed up with pride?
- Am I selfish, thinking it's all about me?
- Am I easily angered?
- Do I love seeing people fall?
- Am I unforgiving?
- Do I keep record of all the hurt and wrong done to me? This question is not asking if you remember the wrong. It's asking can you know types of hurt done to your or can count the numbers of times he or she has wronged you? If so, this is what Paul is referring to when he says, "Love keeps no record."
- Am I childish and immature?
- Do I throw temper tantrum when things don't go my way?
- Am I needed?

If you answered "Yes" to any of the following questions, you need to work on that area immediately. For these things are the opposite of love. Anything that is opposite of love, if not removed will become a stronghold in your life and a dangerous explosive in your marriage or any relationship.

You and God only know how strong and deep rooted these things are in your life. Therefore, you may have to avoid focusing on marriage until after these things are conquered in you. Unlovable things in our lives do not hurt us only, but others. Sometimes the hurt happens with and without your permission and it occurs when you least expect.

A good place to learn about love is in I Corinthians 13. If you have trouble understanding or need guidance, seek counsel from your Church School Teacher or Pastor.

1. Always work hard to improve your marriage.

2. Develop your own relationship with God.

3. Identify and Establish roles.

4. Talk about the finances together.

5. List your non-negotiables; those things you are not willing to give up.

A MARITAL WORKOUT!

(This workout section may start with one spouse, but should always conclude with both spouses doing the workout.)

PRE-MARITAL CHECK LIST

1. Is God first in my life?
   _____

2. Am I seeking Holy Matrimony after I say, "I DO"?
   _____

3. Am I ready for marriage?
   _____
   _____

4. What is my definition of marriage?
   _____
   _____

5. Am I ready to answer to another person?
   _____

6. Am I ready to share all of me with another person?
   _____

7. Am I ready to spend the rest of my life committed to loving one person?
   _____
   _____
   _____

8. Am I a quick forgiver?
   _____

9. What are my non-negotiables?
   _____
   _____
   _____
   _____

10. Am I ready to put someone before myself?
    _____

11. Have I fully recovered from the hurt and pain from my previous relationship?
    _____
    _____

12. Do I still have intimate feelings for my last companion? _____

13. Am I currently dating several people physically, mentally and emotionally?
    _____
    _____
    _____

14. Do I have some RED FLAGS, I need to deal with in my life?
    _____
    _____

If so, what?

_____

_____

15. Do I see some RED FLAGS, in my companion's life, I need to address?

_____

If so, what?

_____

_____

_____

16. Do I want to marry someone with children?

_____

17. Am I willing to be a step-parent?

_____

_____

18. Can I love someone who has been previously married?_____

19. Date of acknowledgement.

_____

20. I have set a goal date to correct what I need to correct.

_____

_____

21. Does my companion put God first?

    _____

22. I have set a date to discuss these issues with my companion.

    _____

    _____

23. My companion and I have set a date to start working on this particular area together.

    _____

    _____

24. How can your companion improve in this particular area?_____

    _____

    _____

25. More examples?

    _____

    _____

26. What do you suggest your companion work to improve on prior to saying "I DO?"_____

    _____

27. Why?

    _____

    _____

28. **Date of acknowledgement.**

_____

_____

29. **Do you need to seek outside guidance?**

_____

30. **If so, when, who and where?**

_____

_____

31. **On today my companion and I accomplished this goal together.**

_____

SPECIAL NOTES:

GET A MOUNTAINTOP MARRIAGE

Matt. 5:1-2 "And seeing the multitude, He went up on a mountain, and when he was seated His disciples came to Him. Then He opened His mouth and taught them."

It's time to take cover and get to your appointed mountain of love. You don't have time to waste. It's urgent that you work at getting there. God has a purpose and plan for your marriage. He wants to get you to the mountain top.

We have read often in the Word of God where Jesus often went to a mountain to pray, receive from God, and to move to a higher place in Holy Matrimony. Where you are at may be good, yet it can get better. What God desires to do in your marriage is far greater than what He has accomplished in it yesterday. However, you must see the need to move and have the willingness to move up to the next level. God has called you to a mountain and it is no place for those who fear heights.

If Jesus saw the need to "Go to the mountain to pray" you and your spouse must do the same. Matt. 5:1-2 "And seeing the multitude, He went up on a mountain, and when he was seated His disciples came to Him. Then He opened His mouth and taught them."

The multitude that was surrounding Jesus, were at a lower level. Jesus wanted to see who really wanted to be a

disciple, who really wanted to come up after Him, hear the truths, and received the deeper things of God. Therefore, He went up a little bit higher on the mountain, sat down and taught what become known as "The Sermon on the Mount."
~ Matt. 5-7

KEEP GOING UP.

Don't stop, keep going up. You have to move up from here and go up a little higher. For you to receive what God has for you, you must go a little further. What you have here is good, but God has so much more for you.

Some of Jesus' most profound teachings couldn't be heard by the people in the city streets or those living down in the valleys. It couldn't be heard by the average, everyday person. Only those who would go up a little higher, climb a little farther and take the time, effort, and pain to push through the challenges and climb the mountain heard it.

"When He had sent the multitudes away, He went up on the mountain by Himself to pray." Now when evening came, he was alone there. Marriage is where two individuals have become one. The oneness that God has blessed your union with should lead the two to position themselves together as one in prayer, in one place at the same time praying for the same thing. It doesn't do the marriage any good if the pray request to God is not unified. When couples admit their need for God and know what they are in need of, they should go to God together. This let God know that you are in agreement as husband and wife. It also let the spouse know, you are touching and agreeing on what is being prayed for. I have spoken to many couples who love communing with God in prayer for their marriage and certain situations. However, as they discuss their prayer request with one another, they soon discover they were both praying for the same things, yet for a different outcome. No marriage God has joined together can survive without prayer.

Since God is the one who join the two together, why not take the marriage back to him regarding anything pertaining to the union. This means not only talk to God when problems arise or when you need a financial breakthrough or increase. Seek God's purpose and direction for the marriage. This should be done when things are going well, not when it seems to unravel at the seams or need repairing. It would be good if every couple and persons find a place where they can get alone with God.

Jesus, himself needed some alone time with God, therefore, He sent the crowds away. Often when we need that alone time, we may have to send everyone away, even our children, parents, best friends, to get up on the top of the mountain to pray. This verse says, "He was alone there."

Where do you go to be alone with God? When it seems as though you are in a rough patch or a pulling in your spirit for the need to move beyond better in your marriage, where do you go or turn to reach that higher or deeper place? I'm not simply speaking about a physical place, although it takes that sometimes. But I'm referring to your spiritual renewal in your marriage. Is God still the center of your joy in your marriage? Is He still viewed as the One with authority of your marriage? Is God still the One who you desire to keep your marriage together and long for His presence? Are you still expecting God to move in and through your marriage or have you become comfortable where you are? God wants to move you from that mountain of your current to the mountain of your future. The new mountain He has for you is obtainable. You can get to that "mountain-top." Ask yourself, 'Is our spirit where God want it to be for the two of us?'

If we want intimacy in our relationship and that power from heaven, we've got to follow Jesus' example: He went to the mountain alone.

Matt. 15:29-30 says "Jesus departed from there, skirted the Sea of Galilee, and went up on the mountain and sat down there. Then great multitudes came to Him, having with them the lame, blind, mute, maimed, and many others; and they laid them down at Jesus' feet, and He healed them." Someone may be asking themselves; how do you get the power to heal what is broken in them or their spouse? The answer is you spend a night on the mountain with God.

When you have a known problem or something which has the potential of causing a problem later, that is the time to seek help, even if that means seeking outside help from your pastor, certified therapist or counselor. Don't avoid the matter with a congestive calendar of things to do. Your marriage is and should always be first priority.

Ask yourself, "How do I go to work all day, be a good husband or wife, take care of our kids, coach the little league team, fulfill other responsibilities and yet, find no time to address marital matters. Avoiding the matter only causes things to fester and become more than what it should be. When a spouse knows of a problem but refuses to address it, causes them resentment toward their mate, a lack of trust, closed communication, and the possibility of infidelity. When one chooses to ignore or discuss with their spouse what is bothering them, it becomes like yeast in dough. The longer you let it sit, the more it swells.

Talking about marital problems is very crucial. The person being viewed in a certain way may not know there is a problem, until you tell them. Most times, couples wait until the mole hill becomes a mountain before they see the need to talk, in which then the problem is out of control. The verbiage and tone become unpleasant toward the other one. Avoiding a problem doesn't send the problem away. It just leaves it to lay dormant for resentment and bitterness to sit it. When this happens, this is time to get to the top of the mountain. At the top of a mountain is where you saw, heard and gained holy boldness in Christ Jesus. On the mountain top, God gave strong lessons regarding relationship.

CLEAR VISION

I am a witness that when you get up on that mountaintop and spend some time alone with God, the vision for your marriage will become clearer. God will speak to you and show you how to address the issue at hand. Often, in a relationship we want to handle matters according to our feelings. However, God wants us to handle matters with peace.

Then, when the multitude or mob shows up those who we call family, friends, co-workers, telling you what you already know, you will be ready for them. There is nothing like having a mob that only supports one person in the marriage and resents the other one. This support group is unhealthy and dangerous for any marriage. When trouble arises, because they dislike the spouse, they will not hear the wrong in you, when telling them of your problem. Having the wrong support group can be additional trouble you don't need in your marriage.

Often, we get burned out with each other in a marriage, because we're trying to work, manage a family, volunteer, handle church, continue your education and or start up a new business. Due to the many soils we sink our hands into we become stressful with everything making demands on our time. When this happens, we don't have time to seek God, even in ministry. All we know is we have to complete this assignment. It's possible to be so busy that you allow your seeking of God to take the back seat. You can become so fixed on completing a task you fail to seek the One who gave you the assignment. All we know is, we don't have time to go to the mountain to be alone with God. We tell ourselves "He is with me, always," yet, doing your own thing.

We have not only the stress of the world, but we have disconnected from our Power Source! Let me be the first to warn you, the problem is not that we can afford to give time to God, we don't have time to exclude Him. We need Him in our lives as individuals, so that He may exist in our marriage.

I recall one professor saying, "I'm so busy today, and there is so much on my schedule that I'm going to take an extra hour and pray." Most time what we say is "I'm so busy and have so much on my calendar today. I'll pray in my car on my way to the meeting, to work." Time with God can happen in those places, however time with God should be on purpose and intentional, not on the fly by. Many people operate in ministry by the fly of the seat of their pants. This should not be in a marriage.

It's great to pray in the car. That's better than getting mad at everyone around you. But never take the attitude that you don't have to make time to pray or think that you don't need or have time to pray. When you stop praying, you disconnect from the very source of what you need.

The way Jesus prepared for the multitudes that came with all their diseases, pains, and problems was to find a place on the mountain where He could be alone to commune with God…

Regardless, if you are in your living room, backyard, your camper or your prayer closet, everyone needs a War ROOM, where they can cry out to God. I remember my dad telling me, "Just a little talk with the Father will make everything okay." Jesus felt the need to talk to His Father, so, He went up a little higher. There are things you can't do or get on the lower level. You must go up a little higher. Jesus ascended after the crucifixion from the Mount of Olives, and He will descend to that same mount at the Second Coming.

One course I had to take in school was Ancient Middle East. I recall studying the Mount of Olive, a mountain outside the city of Jesus. From this mountain, you could see the walls in various parts of the city, and nearby was an olive grove; which is why they called it "Mount Olive." Jerusalem itself is located at about 2,000 feet above sea level, settled in several hills. This reminded me of the many spiritual things that took place on Jerusalem's mountaintops: Moses received the Law, Elijah defeated Baal, and Jesus communed with God.

Jerusalem was right outside the city of Golgotha, the same mountain where Jesus was crucified. In Jerusalem there are many mountains to see, because Israel is a very mountainous region. When you go up to the Sea of Galilee, there are mountains all around. Throughout the Bible you read about the Holy Hill, Mount Zion, where Jerusalem is located. The mountains declare the glory of God. God dwells in His Mountains and He does a lot of His best work there.

GET ON THE TOP OF THE MOUNTAIN

It's good when you can look at your spouse and say, "Let's get on top the Mountain." I often tell myself and others to, "Meet me at the top, because I won't be at the bottom." Your marriage is a few steps away from being on top of where God has called you to be. No matter what you are going through or trying to accomplish in your marriage, you must see yourselves on top of it or working toward getting there. Whether it is your finances, purchasing a new home, going on that dream vacation, becoming better communicators with one another, forgiveness… you must see yourselves on top. Seeing things only from its rawness can be discouraging, because you are looking at what it is. However, when you view it from the top, you see what it shall be.

Are you willing to allow God to call your marriage up to the mountain? Or are you comfortable and stuck living in the valley? If you've been right there for over seven days, you've been there long enough. It's time to plan for day eight. Day eight God will do a new thing. Therefore, it's time to prepare yourself to start a new beginning. It is very vital for you to spend time celebrating, but you don't want to spend the rest of your life celebrating that one thing when you have so much more to accomplish. If you are at a point in your marriage where mistakes have happened, love is dampened and what once was gleam is dull, you can't keep letting that part of life beat you down, when God wants you to come on up. Why, because you have HIS WORD and YOU HAVE HIS POWER. Now, all you just have to do is receive it within and express it outwardly toward one another.

When God calls us to a mountain it means He plans to meet us up there, to teach us and lift us up in His glory. A glorious time is what God has in mind for us on the mountain, which means we've got to be willing to put in the work of climbing up a little higher. Some mountains will take longer than others, yet if God calls you there, He will empower you to get there only if you are up for the challenge. No marriage is perfect. They all have its ups and downs. Therefore, we can't settle for life in the low lands or at the base of the mountains nursing and rehearsing the woes of what went wrong. We must view the errors and let them be lessons for the future. Staying in the low lands of hurt and pain keeps you down in the dump or a place whereby the scavengers, serpents, and buzzards can constantly eat at your love for one another.

If you don't mind me meddling for a moment, tell me; what kind of person are you? Are you a mountain climber? Are you willing to try climbing? If you could go to Mount Rainier, would you be standing at the foot of mountain looking up at it and wonders what it would be like to be up on the top of it; OR, are you one who would gear up with the tools you need to climb up the mountain. Asking God for strength to climb is a power tool you can't do without in order to actually climb up that Mountain.

I know many people like speaking to their mountain and making it disappear, because some mountains needs to be removed in our lives. However, there are mountains we are to stand on.

You have to decide, where you will stand. You have the choice of standing at the foot of the mountain or standing on top of the mountain. The choice is yours. Now, it would be good if one person can make it to the top, but it's better when you and your spouse make it to the top together. When one is standing on top and the other one is left at the bottom it can become very uncomfortable and lonely for the one left at the bottom. No one likes feeling left behind. Yet the person on top may feel like a brand-new person. Why, because they know what it is like being down there at the bottom.

The longer the person is at the bottom, the more they lack the experience of being on top of that mountain with you, the more resentful they may become. Being on top of a mountain is not a place you want to be alone. You need your spouse beside you to help keep you balanced. I'm not talking about a physical mountain, because who cares whether you ever go up in the natural or not? I'm talking about climbing up in your attitude toward life and the experience of life. Jesus said, "I come that you might have life and have it more abundantly." God has many plans for your marriage; however, you must put in the work to receive them.

This life called marriage is not a rehearsal. It's real and has the potential of helping or hurting more than just the two who said, "I Do." We all have been given one life to live and when it's over it's over. So, is your marriage, whether you have filed for divorce or not. You don't get a do over. This is no practice run. Marriage is always in the real time, even if you get a divorce and remarry the same spouse, it's not a practice. Therefore, you ought to live each day to the maximum, by seizing every moment. One of the joys of being married is the challenge of making your spouse happier than the day before. Happiness need not be expensive, but it just requires time and dedication to one another.

Are you going to be the one who climbs the mountain to be the husband, wife, or servant' to your spouse God wants you to be or are you going to be the person who spends their life in WONDERLAND? Are you going to be satisfied with wondering what it would be like to have a healthy marriage, family and fulfilling life blessed by God; or are you going to have that family with the blessing of God? Are you going to wonder what it would be like to have the faith of God in that thing he's been telling you do; or re you going to climb up a little higher to build the business and ministry that God has put in you? Are you going keep wondering around only building everyone else's dreams, business and ministry while neglecting what God has put in you?

"I have given you every spirit blessing in the heavenly realm." For you to see and do what God has required of you, you must climb up higher and stir up the gift within you. Again, are you going to climb up to your mountaintop or are you going to keep wondering around the base of the mountain looking up, wondering what it would be like to be at the top. Often Wayne and I sit and talk about how far God has brought our marriage. We ministered to each other by saying God has bought us to such a place and time as this. It is at that moment, that we rejoiced and moved toward the top of the mountain.

We never become comfortable with one experience on the mountain. Wayne and I have made it a lifestyle and we are loving it. We love how God allows us to move in His time, and we love it even more when we hear His command to move. I am feeling a mighty move in your life. I hear God telling you right now to move and transition from your current place to the mountain He has appointed you to. Is it forgiveness, spending more time together, communicating, vacationing, etc. with the direction of God ordering your steps, only you and your spouse know which mountain you need to get on top of?

PUT IN THE WORK

Having the desire and will power to climb, is nothing like the actual climb. To get to the top of your mountain together, you must climb up the mountain together simultaneously. Therefore, when one begins to lose strength, they will have the order one's assistance to help pull them up. An uphill climb with an incline is never easy or comfortable, but it's possible. An upward journey sometimes comes with a high incline. Each time God appoints you to a mountain, each one of your climbing days will require effort, which says I will try the climb. It will also require one to exercise their faith and finally it requires endurance that says keep going we're not there yet.

WIDEN YOUR VISION FOR YOUR MARRIAGE

This means you may have to change your current lens for a wider lens. God wants to you see much more for your marriage than what you have been viewing. Therefore, you have to throw away those outdated bifocals and get you a telescope made by God, whereby you can see what He has to show you. Matthew 26:30 says, "And when they had sung a hymn 'this was after the Lord's Supper], they went out to the Mount of Olives. That's where Jesus was arrested. And "Matthew 28:16 "Then the eleven disciples went away into Galilee, to the mountain which Jesus had appointed for them."

I love this scripture. I have read it often, but never have I understood it as I do now. This has never been a memory verse for me to quote later in a class recital, but I love it. The eleven disciples went to the mountain which Jesus had appointed for them. When I read this, God immediately showed me that our marriage doesn't have to be like everyone else's for it to be blessed. God showed me He has special blessings specifically for our marriage. The mountain he appointed Wayne and myself to was a mountain that was tailor made just for us.

God is doing the same things with your marriage. He is appointing you to a mountain tailored made for your marriage. It's a mountain prepared for you and your spouse; you just have to get there. He is waiting on you to show up. He is waiting to meet you there, whereby you can get more serious with Him and your spouse. Something wonderful will happen on the mountain. God will allow you, just as He did Moses. God will allow you as He did Moses to have a transformation and a transfiguration of your own marriage, which is why you can't give up or quit now. You have come too far, to not get your blessing. It's time in your marriage you and your spouse live and serve one another from a higher level. This happens when you are determined to change more than your physical address. A physical change will not get you there alone. What God desires to do in your relationship requires that He does it on the inside of you.

TALK TO YOURSELF

AM I willing to climb up the mountain which God He has appointed for our marriage?

AM I willing to climb up it, step by step, because I can't hurry God by skipping steps or taking short cuts?

AM I ready to get my marriage out the normalcy of an everyday hum drum routine? Believe me, it gets better than that.

AM I willing to go to another level to meet God and find that higher place He has planned for me?

No one can accidently have a relationship someone. Relationships are intentional, whether it is good or bad. You can't slip in spending time with God at the "half-time" report; you must purposely make time for Him. Slipping a little time in for God after you get done with everything else you want to do is not how to go; you must make time for Him. You can't just fit God into a little piece of your little world saying, "Okay, Lord, here I am. Come on and show me your stuff for me." You have to go to the mountain He has appointed for you and meet Him there. Then allow God to do His work in you. God has a plan to transfigure, transform, and translate the vision He has given you for your marriage. When you get on a mountain with God, you get a bigger vision for your life. You will begin to see further than what you've been seeing. Many prays the Jabez prayer "Lord, enlarge my territory," this may include a better vision for your future.

Do you believe God for something in your marriage? If so, what? Perhaps you're saying, "If only we could pay this month's rent without a struggle or borrowing." I dare you to ask God for a blessing to be debt free and make you a Lender. God has the power to give you a vision to see beyond this month once you get on the mountain with Him. You have to be willing to move up from seeing where you are currently at to when you could be. God knows how to translate, transform and transfigure what you see into what He wants you to see and possess. Are you ready to move up?

What are you looking at? "I'm just trusting God to give me enough money for a little piece of car to get me back and forth to work." Rather, try asking God for a vehicle to travel from state to state. It's time for you to look up beyond what you are used to seeing. For you to see further, you must allow God to stretch your vision. There is more life out there than what you are looking at. If all you can see is your past and current, your vision is too small for your life and your marriage. Having monies to retire is good, but what are you doing until you get there? If you do nothing between your now and retiring you will retire before you retire. You will quit and give up, because life has become dull and boring.

The disciples heard the call to the top of the mountain which Jesus had appointed for them and looked what happened after they answer the call?

"When they saw Him, they worshipped Him; but some doubted." And Jesus came and spoke to them, saying "All authority has been given to Me in Heaven and on earth. "Go, therefore, and make disciples of all the nations, baptizing them in the name of the Father and of the Son and of the Holy Spirit, teaching them to observe all things that I have commanded you; and lo I will be with you always, even to the end of the world." ~ Matt. 28:17-20

It is possible that once you arrive to the place God has appointed for you to have one who worship God and one who has doubt. Notice, it says "Some doubted." If one person in the marriage have doubt, that is a blessing, that means the other ones has faith and God can work with that. Just because some doubted, didn't prevent God from speaking of His worldwide power or from giving the disciples His command. Sometimes, only one person in the marriage believes if one person has faith, it is enough for the one to pull them both up to where God wants them to be. The climb up doesn't stop because of the lack of faith in one; it just means the climb has gotten rough. Hearing these words from a mountain climber, I will tell you, "Climbing up the mountain has never been easy, yet it's possible." There are people I will never travel with due to their negativity and doubts. Yet, in my marriage, Wayne and I are determined to have an upward climb, even when one is in doubt. We refuse to leave the other one behind or travel alone. We both know that what God has for our marriage is not just for one to experience.

LIVING IN THE SPIRIT OF UNITY
(How can two walk together unless they be in agreement.)

Unity is a rare and precious jewel needed whenever there's more than one person gathering. This is very important in a marriage. Living as one after you have said I do is different from living together as one before your vows. When a couple lives together before one, there is really no commitment. When things go wrong, the scenery, something or someone better looking or successful comes along or if relationship becomes stale, one has the liberty to walk away, because there was no lifetime commitment to the relationship.

In a loving marriage, walking away is difficult. When the marriage is challenged with disunity, conflict, confusion, chaos, and disagreement, the husband or wife can't just walk away from one another, because vows of commitment are involved. True love endures forever regardless of the many obstacles it must climb. As with any loving marriage, many things come with it. It has to consider a lot of things, situations, circumstances, and people. Couples must understand their relationships involve more than just themselves. Yet, no one wants to or should live a life in disarray with things and people constantly breaking the bond of unity.

When unity is absent, the home becomes disrupted. Just as unity has a major role in the Body of Christ and it determines the outcome of its functions, so it is in the marriage. We all heard the saying, "United we stand; Divided we fall," this is true in every aspect of relationships, especially in a marriage. We have a mandate from the Word of God to be a specific kind of church to glorify Christ. When we understand that people are the church and not the brick and not the place where we assemble to worship, it will take on a different meaning, in our homes and yes in our marriage.

In order for a marriage to glorify God, it must look, talk and walk like God the Father, God the Son, and God the Holy Spirit. We need one another in order for the marriage to work and each person must do his or her part to keep the unity in the marriage. When we live in unity, we reflect the perfect relationship in the Godhead: Father, Son, and Holy Spirit. As husbands and wives, we are connected with the Godhead, which makes us one in spirit, one in purpose, one in passion, all for the Kingdom of God. If each person in the marriage focuses only on their own private agendas, goals, or dreams, then how can the marriage move forward and flourish into Holy Matrimony?

Paul was compelled to write to the Christians at Corinth regarding their gifts. As it is today, some were allowing their gifts to cause disharmony in the Body of Christ. It was very important that he reminded the church about its unity and the diversity within the body. Husband and wives are two different individuals gifted to do what God has called him and her to do. God identifies the female in the marriage as the [Helper, Suitable help meet]. But for Adam there was not found a helper comparable to him. ~Gen. 2:20 The male in the in the marriage is called the "The husband, The Head" ~Eph.5:25:25-29 25 Husbands, love your wives, just as Christ also loved the church and gave Himself for her, 26 that He might sanctify and cleanse her with the washing of water by the word, 27 that He might present her to Himself a glorious church, not having spot or wrinkle or any such thing, but that she should be holy and without blemish. 28 So husbands ought to love their own wives as their own bodies; he who loves his wife loves himself. 29 For no one ever hated his own flesh, but nourishes and cherishes it, just as the Lord does the church.

When God performed his first marriage, he gave each individual a gift and with the gift were attached responsibilities. God expects a return on the gifts he distributed in the couple. One had the gift to help and the other one had the gift to love and lead. The two gifts must never come into conflict.

The husband is not expected to perform the duties of the wife and vice versa. Each has a specific role given to them by God. "Then the LORD God said, "It is not good that the man should be alone." Then God immediately solved that problem. "I will make him a helper fit for him." Eve solved what Adam was lacking. The second important Hebrew word in this verse, translated "fit" is kenegdow. It literally means "according to the opposite of him." God created two individuals perfect for each other. Eve was not created to serve above or beneath Adam. Adam was not presented to lord over his Eve. God did an excellent job at joining Eve with Adam. She was not created to be superior or inferior to Adam. She was created and gifted to compliment his very existence. He provided for her and loved every part of her, which means flaws and all. However, even though one may not have the gift to perform the other person duties, it doesn't mean they can't. The wife can love her husband and the husband can help his wife. This is how the marriage ministry is expected to operate. When husbands and wives come together and function as one, it shows forth the glory and knowledge of God. What they have been given by God for the marriage must work together as one.

In a marriage, each person must remember that regardless, as to what gifts one has been gifted with it comes from God, through The Holy Spirit. The Spiritual Gifts of God doesn't have a better than thou attitude, neither does it operates as such in the marriage. Paul had to set the record straight. "11 But one and the same Spirit works all these things, distributing to each one individually as He wills.

Meaning He don't have to ask for our permission or approval. Paul went further to explain, using the analogy of the body. He said 12 For as the body is one and has many members [diversity], but all the members of that one body, being many, are one body, so also is Christ. 13 For by one Spirit we were all baptized into one body—whether Jews or Greeks, whether slaves or free—and have all been made to drink into one Spirit.

As husband and wife, [Children of God] be "be eager to maintain the unity of the Spirit in the bond of peace" Eph. 4:3. We both have been gifted by the Holy Spirit to serve one another with unity. Therefore, it is up to the individuals as to whether or not, they keep it. The Holy Spirit is the great giver of unity. As husband and wife, we ought to have a goal to live a life of unity.

The Goal of Unity

Everything we do in life should have a goal attached to it, including our marriage. The Goal of Unity in your marriage should be to receive what God has for us on the inside flow into our spouse. This happens when we will have a selfless marriage that serves one another. When unity is present it has a way of shaping two souls who are Spirit-rooted, manifesting Christ, living a life of truth-cherishing, and humbly-loving each other as one. The union and unity that God has for the marriage is designed by Him and has two purposes. For marriage is to be a witness to the world and the manifestation of The Glory of God through the love they have for one another. The apostle John makes the first of these most clear. "A new commandment I give to you, that you love one another: just as I have loved you, you also are to love one another. By this all people will know that you are my disciples, if you have love for one another" ~John 13:34-35.

Jesus' famous statements in John 17 are rooted in the profound spiritual unity between the Father and the Son, and with those whom God has chosen out of the world. John 17:6. "I ask that they may all be one, just as you, Father, are in me, and I in you, that they also may be in us, so that the world may believe that you have sent Me"

The oneness that shines with self-authenticating glory for the world to see is union with the Father and the Son so the glory of the Father and the Son is part of our lives. "The glory that you have given Me I have given to them, that they may be one even as we are one" John 17:22. That glory is knowing this: "I in them and you [The Father] is in Me" John 17:23. From this kind of union with God, and the glory it gives, shines so bright. It is something the world needs to see. God's aim for this vertically-rooted, horizontal, glory-displaying unity is that He might "gather into one, the children of God scattered abroad" John 11:52.

The ultimate goal of such marital unity is to glorify God. Therefore, Paul prays, "May the God of endurance and encouragement grant you to live in such harmony with one another, in accord with Christ Jesus, that together you may with one voice glorify the God and Father of our Lord Jesus Christ. Therefore welcome one another as Christ has welcomed you, for the glory of God" Romans 15:5-7.

Now, how do we get unity in a marriage when it seems that many are clogged up with disharmony? "Do not get drunk with wine, for that is debauchery, but be filled with the Spirit" Eph. 5:18. Seek to be led by the Spirit and to bear the fruits of the Spirit. Gal. 58; 22-23. The fruit of the Spirit, which is Love and the Holy Spirit are the spokes in the wheel of a marriage. The Holy Spirit and Love keeps a marriage moving forward. When the Holy Spirit and Love is a stranger to a marriage, individuals will care less about keeping the wheel turning and the unity it builds.

When both are filled with the Holy Spirit, it must be a personal relationship for each person, because it will take each person to do their part to bring about unity. No one person can do it all by themselves. Just as God the Father, The Son and The Holy Spirit, are unified, so must husbands and wives even though they had different functions. Husbands and wives must never allow their gifts or what they possess to become the instruments used to break their oneness or unity.

I recall reading about Mark Twain and how he used to put a dog and a cat in a cage together as an experiment, to see if they could get along. They did; so, he put a bird, pig, and goat in a locked cage, and they too got along fine with only a few minor adjustments. Then he put in three individuals who claimed to have the same faith and hope in the One true in living God; He put a Baptist, a Presbyterian, and a Catholic all in the same building, and soon afterwards, there was not a living thing left in the building. Mr. Twain said every creature would adjust for peace of Unity, but mankind, each person had to have things his or her way.

What this world needs to see in every marriage God has joined is Love, sweet love, and that loves needs to be consistent. Husband and wives are good at coming together as the Body of Christ when it comes to sex. However, they must come together in unity in other things that pertains to the marriage, such as: Finances, Religion, Children, Debts and other family matters. Henry Ford once said, "Coming together is only the beginning. Staying together is progress. Working together is success." When we as husbands and wives get on one accord, then we can make great impact in the world and fulfill the purpose of our marriage. When marriages are on one accord, they can turn this world right side up. When unity is your goal, you ought to be in pursuit of it.

THE PURSUIT OF UNITY

When unity is your goal, you ought to be in: Paul says "until we all attain the unity of the faith and of the knowledge of the Son of God" Eph. 4:13, In other words, the unity we pursue is the unity of the truth of God in every area of the marriage. Christian unity is more than sharing the truth of God's Word, unity is an action. Meaning something must be done. Unity happens in a marriage when individuals give up thinking different but seek being likeminded. Paul compiles the words for common-mindedness in Phil. 2:2. "Complete my joy by being of the same mind, having the same love, being on one accord and of one mind" Everything we do in the marriage must be aligned and line up with Christ. We as couples pray for the marriage it will show their dependence is on the one who joined them. I believe this when I heard my Wayne pray the scripture "May God who give {Kim and I] endurance and encouragement, give us His Spirit to live in unity [harmony] with one another, as we follow Christ Jesus" Rom. 15:5. Each day God grants you to be married and both are above ground, you both should be in pursuit of unity. In a marriage no one wants to hear they have unity and see something else. I believe if unity is present, it should be seen. Show forth the evidence.

The Evidence of Unity

When Unity is within the marriage it is just as it is in the Body of Christ, there will be evidence of "LOVE." Love will reveal a commitment to do good for the family of God; whether you feel like it or not. Gal. 6:10. But, although difficult for diverse people, the experience of Christian unity is more than that. It includes heart of love, which reflects a heart of unity; not just a sacrifice for those you don't like. It is a feeling of endearment. We are to have a heart of love for those who are in the household of faith, our family in Christ Jesus. "Love one another with brotherly affection" Rm. 12:10. You know you have been past from death unto life when you can love your brothers. Love will give you away. Love will cause you to work in the spirit of Unity.

When two individuals are joined in marriage and both have the anointing of the Holy Spirit in them. They will both witness that having the anointing working through one of us, is not as powerful as having the anointing working through the both of us. Unity gives us the power to help us come together to overcome the insurmountable and reach the unachievable. Unity brings to us the power to make the impossible possible and to the bring dreams we have for our marriage into reality.

The calling of every marriage is to be one willing to live in harmony with someone else. Living as one requires working with one heart, one purpose, while having a unified vision that causes each to be joined together. Unity in a marriage tries to not allow unresolved offenses to separate them or hinder them from being one in spirit and purpose.

Unity in a marriage is when each has the attitude, that we can do it together. Unity does not require that each share 50/50 of caring the load. Example: Wayne is not the cook of the family, I am. However, Wayne sometimes goes to the grocery store and/or the person who cleans up as I am cooking. He may fix the Kool-Aid, get glasses out and fill them with ice to make sure we have something to drink when dinner is ready. Again, he is not doing 100% of cooking the dinner, yet he is contributing elements for when we sit down for dinner. He is carrying his load.

Teamwork in a marriage, says we can do it together. When determined to live in the Spirit a life of Unity, then we as couples will experience togetherness as a lifestyle in these areas.

- Praising God together
- Fellowship together
- Standing together
- Following together
- Ministering together
- Sacrificing together
- Praying together
- Agreeing together
- Planting together
- Be quickened together
- Have quality time together
- Financially Together
- Singing together
- Worshipping together
- Flowing together
- Giving together,
- Fighting the enemy together
- Going together
- Serving together
- Suffering together
- Laboring together
- Working together
- Pull resources together
- Living Peaceably together

Having the unity of God allows us to become a marriage binding together in One Love, One Faith and One Baptism. It's time we declare, [make a proclamation] what we need in the marriage is UNITY that brings about oneness, love and peace.

MARRIAGE EVALUATION

1. What are things we can work on in our marriage to make sure we get, have or keep the unity? *(Items)*

   _____
   _____
   _____
   _____
   _____

2. When will we work on improving our unity? *(Plan of Action)*

   _____
   _____
   _____
   _____
   _____

3. When do we expect to have the things listed in #2 completed? *(Date of Completion)*

   _____
   _____
   _____

EATING A HEALTHY DIET.

Developing a healthy diet together is not a bad thing. I know many people don't like the word "Diet." A diet is nothing but a lifestyle. The result of unity produces a healthy lifestyle. One goal of marriage should be to live in the spirit of UNITY. To do so there must be a healthy diet in place. If you want your marriage to continue growing and healthy the two must eat healthy meals produced by God. We become out of shape and unhealthy when we begin eating those things which are popular, but not healthy.

We believe it is important for spouses to eat the same foods or be on the same diet. I know you didn't vow to have the same diet, but eating the same healthy foods can save you both. When the doctor told Wayne to adjust his diet and to cut out fried food, red meat, sodas and carbohydrates, this was beneficial to me. If these things were not good for him, then how could they be good for me? This meant there has to be some adjustments with us both. Just because some is good to us, doesn't mean it's good for us. We are one!

Too often we spend our lives eating things which are not good for our body, because those customs or traditions were passed down to us from generations to generations. Then we justify it by using the scriptures. Most people would agree that physicians are a gift from God, but yet we avoid them. And if we do go visit them, we ignore the instruction they give. Some would even go through taking their prescription to the pharmacy, waiting on it to get filled and spend lots of money to receive it. Yet, they have settled in their mind and have no intentions on taking the medication prescribed just for them and their particular illness.

God is the one who constituted marriage. Therefore, couples need to get and read the manual regarding the upkeep of it. What we should be eating is the WORD OF GOD. God has a plan for each marriage He has joined. Couples joined together by God should never skip a meal. They should make sure they set a time to eat the WORD OF GOD together. Eating the same foods allows the two to grow together as one. "When he said to me, Son of man, eat this scroll I am giving you and fill your stomach with it." So, I ate it, and it tasted as sweet as honey in my mouth." [Ezekiel 3:3]

It's sad, but true some couples not only fail to eat the same thing, but they fail to eat at the same table. If they do, they pick and choose what part of the meal they want to eat, while complaining about it. One person may eat everything on their plate, while giving praise to the cook. I must admit, I am very finicky or meticulous about what I eat. I don't like eating the center of a sandwich or when my foods touch. I don't like leftover foods from the night before. I cannot eat a full plate, so I have downsized my plate to a saucer. However, my husband is the opposite. He comes from a family where food was scarce. Yet, that was opposite with me. We could sometime leave the table with food still left on our plate. Most times what were left behind were our vegetables. I would eat all the meat and left my vegetables either on the plate, if didn't no one else want them.

Until late, I was the same way as an adult. I would fix a nice plate of food, knowing I would not eat it all. My mindset was, "make the plate look pretty with all the fixings on it." Yet, Wayne lived by the law, "If it's on your plate you must eat it all." He can't stand to waste food or purchase food when we have a refrigerator filled with food. To him, it's like having the Word of God on the coffee table, but not reading it. We have the food in the refrigerator, but we are not eating it. Many couples have the Word of God in them, on their coffee table, in their vehicles, on their jobs, etc. Yet they fail to read or apply it.

Couples have the same resources available, but they both fail to utilize them. It's like the evening when supper has not been prepared; "Go for yourself" get whatever satisfies you, rather than getting what's best for the two. What we eat or don't eat today, will have an effect on our bodies tomorrow. Couples may not like the same food they purchase, however, they both should love eating the Word of God together.

Peter's Vision

"No, Lord!" Peter answered, "I have never eaten anything impure or unclean." 15The voice spoke to him a second time: "Do not call anything impure that God has made clean."16This happened three times, and all at once the sheet was taken back up into heaven.… Acts 10:14-16 "A man is not defiled by what enters his mouth, but by what comes out of it." Matthew 15:11 "Because, it does not enter his heart, but it goes into his stomach and then is eliminated." Mark7:19 Thus all foods are clean.

EAT THE SCROLL

Ezekiel 3:3 Then he said to me, "Son of man, eat this scroll I am giving you and fill your stomach with it." So, I ate it, and it tasted as sweet as honey in my mouth."

Thy words were found, and I did eat them; and thy word was unto me the joy and rejoicing of mine heart: for I am called by thy name, O LORD God of. Jer. 15:16 And I went unto the angel, and said unto him, Give me the little book. And he said unto me, Take it, and eat it up" Rev. 10:9-11

There are three times in the Bible where it is recorded that somebody ate the scroll. The scroll containing the word of God. Times of old it wasn't written as it is today. Yet, it is similar or equivalent to what is known to us as the Bible. We have Jeremiah [Jeremiah 15:16], Ezekiel, and John The Revelator [Rev 10:9-11]. The passage on Ezekiel is from Ezekiel 2:8 – Ezekiel 3:3; which is perhaps the most detailed account out of the three. The old question is, did Ezekiel really eat the scroll? If he did, how was it possible? If he didn't, how do you explain Ezekiel 3:2 – So I opened my mouth, and he gave me the scroll to eat? In reading the Bible and trying to make sense of the verses in the Bible, there are two ways to do it – first, by using the literal meaning, second, by using the figurative meaning. I'm no scholar, but I've been taught that whenever possible use the literal meaning to explain the words of the Bible, and if impossible, then take the simple road of explaining it.

You may have to be figurative. The books of Revelations, Ezekiel and Daniel mainly are so written with so much imagery and symbols whereby one has to adopt the figurative meaning. As you read the books of prophets, they do that. It made sense the apostles wrote for the lay Christians and thus used a simplified and common speech; the prophets were largely writing what they saw in their visions, which rarely are meant for all to understand. I will keep it simple as I tackle the act of eating the scroll by its figurative meaning, stay with me.

How does this look for Jeremiah, Ezekiel, and John as they all ate the scroll? Did they put the entire scroll in their mouths at one time? Did they take bites at a time or did they tear it into pieces, swallowed it, and digested it. I am no scholar, and I dare not say they did not eat it. I believe if God can make mountains move and divide seas, God can make His men eat scrolls and still be perfectly healthy. I know someone may be wondering and asking themselves. What does it mean to eat scrolls? I understand moving mountains and dividing seas, but eating scrolls seems to be a bit too much? Is this healthy? Is it necessary? There is no literal meaning to be derived from such an act. The only meaning in the figurative and symbolic meaning of such an act, which is a great meaning. So, whether or not you agree with me these three men did not literally eat the scrolls or not, it probably is hard to argue against the need to use the figurative meaning of such an act.

Chew Your Food

Unless you are created with special abilities, I'm sure you eat things in the same way as I do. You pick up your food and place it in your mouth; then you bite it into pieces and chew on it repeatedly to easily digest it; then you swallow it, it goes through your gullet and into your stomachs where it gets digested. Well, that's as much as I remember from biology class a long time ago. I can be corrected later, if I am wrong. It's the same thing with the Word of God. You pick up God's words and you read it. You meditate on it repeatedly until you understand it or receive something from it – you digest it, and apply it in your daily life, living it out, and letting aspects of your being soak in God's truths. Try this and when you do, afterwards you will learn even you can eat a scroll.

Why The Scroll?

What is a scroll? In Ezekiel 2:10 – On both sides of it were written words of lament and mourning and woe. The scroll was loaded with God's words. Today, we call it by its ancient term the Bible, The Word of God.

When Ezekiel ate it, it tasted as sweet as honey in his mouth. We are encouraged to load our mouths with God's words. God's Words are sweet and the taste last forever. The Word of God has no expiration date. The sweetest taste in my mouth has been when I first ate the word of God. I must admit I have had a sweet tooth ever since. This sweetness comes when we learn to understand God's precepts, for ourselves. Daddy, momma, our pastor, and Sunday School

Teachers are good with explaining the Word, but when I searched it, meditating on it and believing it myself, the more my soul hungered for it and the sweeter it became. This allows you to become greatly satisfied as you stand marveling at the greatness of God and His Kingdom. Hearing the Words of The Psalmist as he proclaims, "How sweet are your words to my taste, sweeter than honey to my mouth!" [Psalm 119:103] are mouth filling words. When Wayne and I disagree, we allow the Words of God to feed us and shape our words toward one another. This keeps us from saying that hurts the other one, which hinders us from glorifying God with our words. I have witnessed how bad or poor choice of words leads to bad and poor choices in a relationship, including a marriage.

Everyone knows we love sweets. Wayne loves cakes, cookies and pies, while myself I love those hard candies like Jolly Ranchers, Laffy Taffy, Now & Laters, etc. Ezekiel, had a sweet taste in his mouth, which prompts me to wonder what was the aftertaste like? I wonder what the Word tasted like, after he swallowed it. Ezekiel did not include the answer in his telling of it. Yet, we can find a descriptive account of the taste in Revelation. In Revelation 10:9, the angel told John that the scroll will turn John's stomach sour, but in his mouth, it will be as sweet as honey. As we continue reading, the next verse says John ate it and "It tasted as sweet as honey in my mouth, but when I had eaten it, my stomach turned sour." [Rev 10:10]. My referencing the verses in Revelation to prove God's Word is consistent. God's words will always be sweet at first when you first understand and connect with it. It's when you apply it, you will find your stomach turning sour. We love the Word of God, but don't always like what it tells us, especially when we know we are wrong or want to do harm to others. Likewise, in the beginning of a relationship or marriage, everything is sweet, until things don't go in our favor. We sometimes say things in the heat of the moment or express those things we've been storing up to one day get off our chest. When we do this, we say things which make the situation and/or person stomach sour. However, our words have a way of turning our stomach sours. When this happens, we risk losing a lot. We develop a sour stomach when one uses words not of Godly and if they are of God, they are not always used with the Spirit of God or we use them at the wrong time.

In the heat of the battle or conversation, pause a moment to ask yourself, "What would Jesus say?" If you cannot find the right things let me give you this line, "Can we table this conversation to another day?" Then set a date and time to convene the conversation. God's Words are sweet to listen to, sour to follow, but produces great results and is fitting for every situation. Another example is when you are out on a date or being intimate, these are not the right time to pull out the rod of correction regarding something your spouse may need to do. You can say the right thing, the right way, but at the wrong moment.

In order to experience Holy Matrimony, we need to eat God's words, and even those who think they don't need it or like it. The Word should be our daily bread. God Word is our spiritual food which is our source of energy. The Word is a necessity for our marriage. We can't survive or last without it. It is our compass. It's like food and water, we cannot live without it consistently. We must have the Word of God daily and several helping a day. You may call us greedy, but we have to have it more than once a week in church, not once a day, but constantly throughout each day. Examine your marriage and ask yourself, "Are we eating the Words of God allowing it to digest? Or are you sniffing it before you eat it to determine whether or not you eat it? Are you anorexic? Are you eating the Word of God, but vomiting it out after eating it? Are you picky with the words that you eat, ignoring those that do not wet your appetite? If you have been eating the words of God properly, there will be spiritual growth. Might not be immediately obvious, of course, but if you keep eating God's words, keep digesting them, keep living them out – surely, one day, even if you don't notice it yourself, someone will come up and let you know that, hey, you've changed. After eating God's words, you are expected to do something about it – the three men were told to preach and prophesy [Rev 10:11, Ezekiel 3:4]. And as for us, let us do what we can, let us do what we must, and let us begin by eating the word of God for our marriage.

Soul Foods to EAT

(Gal. 5:22-23) Godly Marriages are produced by the Holy Spirit; not by self-effort.

Love (I Cor. 13; 1 John 3:16 "We know we have been past from death until life, because we have love for one another; Rom. 13:9-10 "Love your neighbor as you love yourself. Love don't hurt or harm his neighbor. Love is obeying the law.) Love all people (Matt. 5:43-44) Love all people. "Love your neighbor and hate your enemies, but I say to you, love your enemies. Pray for those who hurt you. IF you do this you will be true children of your Father in Heaven. He causes the sun to rise on good and evil people. And he sends rain to those who do right and to those who do wrong.

Joy (I Chron. 29:22 "They ate and drank with great joy in the presence of the LORD that day. Then they acknowledged Solomon, son of David, as king, a second time, anointing him before the LORD to be ruler and Zadok to be priest."; Nehemiah 8:10 "Nehemiah said, "Go and enjoy choice food and sweet drinks, and send some to those who have nothing prepared. This day is holy to our Lord. Do not grieve, for the joy of the LORD is your strength.") What you consume should become a blessing to you and others.)

Peace (Is. 26:3 "He will keep you in perfect peace, when you keep your mind on Him."; John 14:27 "Peace I leave with you; my peace I give you. I do not give to you as the world gives. Do not let your hearts be troubled and do not be afraid."; Rom. 5:1 "Therefore, since we have been justified through faith, we[a] have peace with God through our Lord Jesus Christ,"; Col. 3:15 "Let the peace of Christ rule in your hearts, since as members of one body you were called to peace. And be thankful.")

Patience -able to handle pain or difficult times calmly and without complaining. Patience will teach you how to WAIT ON GOD.

Rom. 12:12 "Be joyful because you have hope. Be patient when trouble comes, and pray at all times. Share with God's people who need help. Bring strangers in need into your homes."

Patience is a command: Eph. 4:2 "Always be humble, gentle and patient, accepting one another in love." James 5:7 "Be patient until the Lord comes again. A farmer patiently waits for his valuable crop to grow from the earth and for it to receive the autumn and spring rains."

Kindness – (Matt. 5:7 "Blessed are the merciful, for they will be shown mercy towards others;) When you remember how you felt after a person was rude toward you, then it should move you to be kind toward others. Remember, Paul tells us that love is not rude.

Forgiveness: What you have received freely should be what you give. Un-forgiveness has the power to destroy the container. In other words, un-forgiveness only hurts the person that's carrying it. Eph. 2:4-10 "But because of his great love for us, God, who is rich in mercy, 5 made us alive with Christ even when we were dead in transgressions—it is by grace you have been saved. 6 And God raised us up with Christ and seated us with him in the heavenly realms in Christ Jesus, 7 in order that in the coming ages he might show the incomparable riches of his grace, expressed in his kindness to us in Christ Jesus. 8 For it is by grace you have been saved, through faith—and this is not from yourselves, it is the gift of God— 9 not by works, so that no one can boast. 10 For we are God's handiwork, created in Christ

Jesus to do good works, which God prepared in advance for us to do."

Rom. 12:21 Regardless, of what the enemy throws your way, learn to flip the script. "Do not be overcome by evil, but overcome evil with good."

Mark 11:25-26 "And whenever you stand praying, if you have anything against anyone, forgive him; that your Father in heaven may also forgive you your trespasses. But if you do not forgive, neither will your Father in heaven forgive your trespasses."

Matt. 18:15 "If your brother sins against you, go and him his fault between you and him alone. If he hears you, you have gained your brother."

Goodness -PS. 23:6 Goodness and Mercy shall follow me all the days of my life. Do good and it will follow you."

Faithfulness – They people say they have faith: Faith (Heb. 11:1; Heb. 11:6; Faith will keep you grounded. Come what may, you are going to have to have Faith in God at all times. Double-minded person is unstable in all his ways.) Faith (God moves as fast as our faith moves.

Patience: In a marriage you have to be patient with one another. Many finds it easier to be patient with a co-worker, because if not they can lose their job. However, it the same with your marriage. If you are not patient you can lose them. Knowing that the testing of your faith produces patience." ~ James 1:3

Be Strong. Your spouse knows where you are strong and your weakness. They love seeing you operate in your strength and will support it. Yet, they will do whatever it takes to cover your weaknesses, while working to strengthening it. I Cor. 16:13 "Watch, stand fast in the faith be brave, be strong."

Re-adjust your lens. Wherever, you are in your marriage, it's time to move your faith to another level. You don't have to see it, know it or know when that it can get better or change in order for it to happen. II Cor. 5:7 "For we walk by faith, not by sight."

I Tim. 3:9 "Holding the mystery of the faith with a pure conscience."

Rom. 3:30 "Since there is one God who will justify the circumcised by faith and the uncircumcised through faith."

James 1:2 "My Brethren, count it all joy when you fall into various trails."

Luke 17:6 "So the Lord said, "If you have faith the size of the mustard seed, you can say to this mountain (mulberry tree), "be pulled up by the roots and be planted in the sea, and it would obey you."

Eph. 4:13 "Til we all come into the unity of faith and of the knowledge of the Son of God, to a perfect man, to the measure of the stature of the fullness of Christ."

Rom. 12:3 "For I say, though the Grace given to me, to everyone who is among you, not to think of himself more highly than he ought to think, but t think soberly, as God has dealt to each one a measure of Faith. God has given every man a measure of faith."

FAITHFULNESS is evidence of your FAITH (People will be faithful to God, their church, their ministry, on their career and to their spouse. Whatever or whomever you are committed to will be revealed in the hard work that follows the commitment.)

Gentleness – Zach. 9:9; Matt. 11:29. This is not to be confused with firmness or stern. When you are gentle you won't force it. I Peter 3:3-8 "Your beauty should not come from outward adornment, such as elaborate hairstyles and the wearing of gold jewelry or fine clothes. 4 Rather, it should be that of your inner self, the unfading beauty of a gentle and quiet spirit, which is of great worth in God's sight. 5 For this is the way the holy women of the past who put their hope in God used to adorn themselves. They submitted themselves to their own husbands, 6 like Sarah, who obeyed Abraham and called him her lord. You are her daughters if you do what is right and do not give way to fear.

7 Husbands, in the same way be considerate as you live with your wives, and treat them with respect as the weaker partner and as heirs with you of the gracious gift of life, so nothing will hinder your prayers. 8 Finally, all of you, be like-minded, be sympathetic, love one another, be compassionate and humble.

Self-Control – The only person you can control is self and that is a full-time job. (II Tim. 1:7-8 "For the Spirit God gave us does not make us timid, but gives us power, love and self-discipline. 8 So do not be ashamed of the testimony about our Lord or of me his prisoner. Rather, join with me in suffering for the gospel, by the power of God.")

Giving – When you give to your spouse, you should always seek to give as if it's your last time to bless them with your best offering. Remember, giving is not always monetary. (Mk. 12:41-43 "The men of Nineveh will stand up at the judgment with this generation and condemn it; for they repented at the preaching of Jonah, and now something greater than Jonah is here. 42 The Queen of the South will rise at the judgment with this generation and condemn it; for she came from the ends of the earth to listen to Solomon's wisdom, and now something greater than Solomon is here. 43 "When an impure spirit comes out of a person, it goes through arid places seeking rest and does not find it." Matt. 6:19-24 "Do not store up for yourselves treasures on earth, where moths and vermin destroy, and where thieves break in and steal. 20 But store up for yourselves treasures in heaven, where moths and vermin do not destroy, and where thieves do not break in and steal. 21 For where your treasure is, there your heart will be also. 22 "The eye is the lamp of the body. If your eyes are healthy, your whole body will be full of light. 23 But if your eyes are unhealthy, your whole body will be full of darkness. If then the light within you is darkness, how great is that darkness! 24 "No one can serve two masters. Either you will hate the one and love the other, or you will be devoted to the one and despise the other. You cannot serve both God and money."

Holiness – (Rom. 6:22 "But now that you have been set free from sin and have become slaves of God, the benefit you reap leads to holiness, and the result is eternal life. Eph. 4:24 "and to put on the new self, created to be like God in true righteousness and holiness." Heb. 12:10 "They disciplined us for a little while as they thought best; but God disciplines us for our good, in order that we may share in his holiness." Heb. 12:14 "Make every effort to live in peace with everyone and to be holy; without holiness no one will see the Lord."

Righteousness – (Job 37:23 "The Almighty is beyond our reach and exalted in power; in his justice and great righteousness, he does not oppress.; Psalms 7:8 "Let the LORD judge the peoples. Vindicate me, LORD, according to my righteousness, according to my integrity, O Most High. Psalms 7:17 "I will give thanks to the LORD because of his righteousness; I will sing the praises of the name of the LORD Most High." 2 Cor. 5:21"God made him who had no sin to be sin for us, so that in him we might become the righteousness of God.

Honesty (Proverbs 11:1-2 "The LORD detests dishonest scales, but accurate weights find favor with him. 2 When pride comes, then comes disgrace, but with humility comes wisdom.

Work – Work toward correcting what is wrong or needful, because tomorrow may be too late or cost you more. (John 9:4 "As long as it is day, we must do the works of him who sent me. Night is coming, when no one can work.; Js. 1:25 "But whoever looks intently into the perfect law that gives freedom, and continues to lives work and operate in it ~not forgetting what they have heard, but working hard to do it—they will be blessed in what they do.")

Procrastination: God wants to heal, deliver and set your marriage free from anything that has it bound today. If you failed to show your spouse love on yesterday, today is the day to show it. Don't wait until tomorrow or your anniversary. All you have is today. They desire to feel your presence today, after they have messed up yesterday. Ask yourself, "When was the last time I gave my spouse a good rub down, compliment, or words of encouragement. When was the last time I was intimate, romantic, and sexual with my spouse? Remember, it doesn't take long for the enemy to plant a thought on our mind. His plan is to feed our mind with negatives regarding our spouse and what we long for from them. Our body becomes a servant of our mind, shortly after Satan provoke or fill it with his thought. So, give your spouse attention where it is needed, before the enemy creep in. Waiting until tomorrow may be too late. It is important for you to start working immediately after you gain whiff of something that has the potential to cause kayos. Doing what needs to be done today will prepare you for many marital blessing God has prepared to give you on tomorrow. What you know to do should be done today, because today is all we have. Tomorrow is filled with many promises, yet it is no guaranteed you will see tomorrow. In Exodus 10:4 "If you refuse to let them go, I will bring locusts into your country [home, dwellings] tomorrow." Numbers 11:18 "Tell the people: 'Consecrate yourselves in preparation for tomorrow, when you will eat meat. The LORD heard you when you wailed, "If only we had meat to eat! We were better off in Egypt!" Now the LORD will give you meat, and you will eat it." Joshua 7:13 "Go, consecrate the people. Tell them, consecrate yourselves in preparation for tomorrow; for this is what the LORD, the God of Israel, says: There are devoted things among you, Israel. You cannot stand against your enemies until you remove them." Matt. 25:1-5,13 "At that time the kingdom of heaven will be like ten virgins who took their lamps and went out to meet the bridegroom. 2 Five of them were foolish and five were wise. 3 The foolish ones took their lamps but did not take any oil with them. 4 The wise ones, however, took oil in jars along with their lamps. 5 The bridegroom was a long time in coming, and they all became drowsy and fell asleep. 13 "Therefore keep watch, because you do not know the day or the hour.")

Foods to Avoid:

Crunchy Foods: Are only pleasing to the one eating them. They are those unlovable things in a person, but has the tendency to offend others. Things like carrots, chips, crackers are just a few things that crunch. They are loud, noisy, and very offensive to those nearby. You can be saying the right thing, however if you are shouting and screaming no one hears you. People sometimes think they are getting their point across, because they talk loudly, when in reality, they are just making loud noise. It's like a baby who shakes their rattler, just to make noise. Many people's mouths are open and their tongue is moving, yet people are not listening or hearing what is being said, due to the loud high pitch volume. Don't be guilty of not having love in your heart. When love is absent, it will show up in your relationship and other services you try to render and it will have no effect. Likewise, when love is present evidence will come. Everything we do and say toward others should be seasoned with love. A good place to practice not eating crunching foods is in the home. The love you give at home will spill over toward others outside the home. Our love toward one another is proof of our love for God.

Popcorn: They are hard to digest, because of the kernel. Don't last. They will pop in hot and on fire, until they get what they want. They want things immediately. They are the ones you see pop-up overnight. They don't know who they are or what they want to do. They pop up depending how hot the fire. They will tell you they want to be involved, but they when you call on them and hold them accountable. They will pop up and leave, because that Kernel of truth got stuck in their teeth and they couldn't handle it. Popcorn hinders you from being responsible and growing up, because you keep dealing with that Kernel. I don't believe they said…They cause people to wondering, why did they say would, or even volunteer… (Let your Yea, mean Yeah.)

Pork Salt (They are too salty. They are bitter and jealousy and can't stand to see you happy. They can work with you, but they are bitter and jealous of you. They have that Cain and Able spirit.): Salt causes high blood pressure and could lead to a heart attack, aneurism, or stroke. No matter how peaceful it is going, the salty bitter people will disturb your peace. You can have peace and it won't be long before it messes with your body and the peace in the body of Christ.

Sweet and Sour Patches: It looks pleasing to the eyes of those on social media and the public only. The words and portraits you give outside the home are very colorful, versatile. Yet, they become meaningless regarding the vision for your marriage. This food sends mixed messages. One person in the marriage knows that is more going to in the house, than what is being said and done before the public. The mixed behavior of love becomes sour when one is leading them. Things are only sweet when the spotlight is on, yet have a foul mouth when the mass is not looking. Sour patches allow one to be more in turned with having a marriage full of hype rather than a living hope. No one or should I say "It is hard for me to image spending a life with a fairy tale marriage. I want to live in the real, no matter how hard it may be." They are only into the Moment and not the Momentum (The moment, when it our time to shine and when things are going their way). They care less about the momentum. They don't care about the direction of the Lord's vision. They are the authority abusers and will be a person down with their foul mouth. They have influence to invite them when doing something and downplay what the church is doing for the body.

Neck bones, Oxtails, or Black Bass. These foods have lots of bones and very little meat. These foods will cause one to choke from what they are not ready for. Just because one may be able to eat it, does not mean they both can. It's hard to get to the meat, due to the bones. When you leave the conversation and three days later your spouse is still asking the questions "What did you mean," it's because you gave them the bones of your words, yet your words lacked clarity, which is the meat for the bones of what you expected them to understand and digest.

The Bread of Idleness (Ps. 31:27) Sitting around doing nothing. As a husband or wife, you should always seek to find something to do with your time. Whether you are working in the home or outside the home. When the mind is free to do nothing, that is what happens, nothing. Time is so precious and it should not be wasted on nothing. God will bless your hand. Therefore, put your hands to good work and watch the blessings of God spring forth in your marriage. (Deut. 28:8 "The LORD will send a blessing on your barns and on everything you put your hand to. The LORD your God will bless you in the land he is giving you."

A Pure Milk Diet for Life: You have to be gentle with these people. (All they drink is milk: Goat Milk, Condense Milk, Evaporated Milk, Butter Milk. Yes, milk does the body good. However, too much milk can ruin the body, especially the wrong milk which is why some can't drink 100% homogenize milk. Some has become lactose intolerant, whereby you can't handle the simple words of God and will choke off the meat. You can't be too honest with them because it will kill them. 1 Peter 2:2 like newborn babies, long for the pure milk of the word, so that by it you may grow regarding salvation. We can't teach you how to leave righteous, because you are still on the nipple. Too sensitive, you think everyone is jealous of me, talking about me, they won't let me do nothing.

Chewing Gum (Self-Control) – I recall our dentist told us that chewing gum was bad on our teeth. Chewing gum are those foods that cause you to be pulled everywhere, because you have an appetite to what pleases the ear. They are blown away with every wind of doctrine. Chewing gum causes you to lose self-control. Before you know it, the gum is making loud sounds, flopping in and out of your mouth. These things irritate others and you become numb to their feelings. At this point, no one can tell you anything, because you don't believe you are doing anything wrong by chewing gum. Don't allow chewing gum to be part of your diet. If it is, spit it out in the toilet or trash can immediately, to avoid causing a mess of getting on your spouse shoes. Then you will have a sticky situation you weren't ready for. Your messiness can provoke or lead your spouse away from you, rather than closer. [Eph. 4:14, II Timothy 4:1-3]

Now and Laters – Stop passing the buck. Admit it and move on. Deal with it now, because tomorrow may be too late. Some people have a way of pointing the finger, while waiting on Nathan to come say, "Thou Art the Man." When you know "it's you" no one should be able to point at you saying, "You're the guilty one." As you receive help for your now situation, you should not procrastinate, apply it now, rather than waiting for a later or the right time. What you ignore today, can be very expensive tomorrow. [Proverbs 24:16, Romans 3:23, Hebrews 6:8]

Cheese. If you have ever been constipated, you will agree it's a terrible feeling. Cheese will lock your bowels up. Nothing is being released and that is how some spouses are. They are not releasing their spouse from the hurt and harm done to them. They are simply constipated. As much as I love eating cheese, I have to admit it will block your colon whereby nothing can be released.

This is true with some marriages. They are clogged up with lots of things whereby nothing can or is passing through their love system. Many are so backed up with waste, which is preventing them from releasing their spouse from the hurt and harm done to them years ago, yet they remain to stay with them. When this happens, someone in the marriage is constipated. They have become a Cheesy Spouse. At least one if not both are all cheesy with smiles in the presence of company or during their Public Display of Affection [PDA] time, but very withdrawn in private. They have forgotten how God forgave them. The cheesy smiles get you high in the spirit and soon as your public appearance is done, you're back to holding on to that one thing you could not pass. They go through life hiding behind the walls of their own home regretting their spouse, being mean toward them, talking about a fakeness of others, being bitter, while blaming everyone for their lack of release. If you are Cheesy. You should allow God's Word and Love to become an enema, whereby you can have a good release from what have you clogged up.

MARRIAGE EVALUATION

1. Are we both eating the scroll?
   _____
   _____

2. If so, are we eating it together?
   _____
   _____

3. Are we understanding what we are eating?
   _____
   _____

4. What can I do to improve in this particular area?
   _____
   _____

5. What can my spouse do to improve in this particular area?
   _____
   _____

6. Are we eating from two different tables?
   _____

_____

_____

If so, is it causing a problem in our marriage?

_____

_____

7. When will we start working on improving our diet? (Plan of Action)

_____

_____

_____

8. What are we lacking in our diet? (Date of Completion)

_____

_____

_____

9. What can we remove from out diet? (*Date of Completion*)

_____

_____

_____

_____

DO A POP-UP

Today, a lot of businesses are doing "Pop Ups." Their business will Pop-up when and where you least expect it. We are good at conducting Pop-Ups. They are fun and surprising to both of us. Down through the years, we have heard many couples, mostly women, who share how they would pop-up on their spouse trying to catch him doing something wrong. Why not, catch them doing something right or needful.

The pop-up we are referring to is the opposite. We suggest doing pop-ups that will bring life or value to the marriage, not those things which have no substance for either person. We believe one should do whatever it takes to make their spouse happy. When couples purposely spend time focusing on pleasing the other person, they will move from distractions of what went wrong.

Many have forgotten how to be spontaneous with one another. Therefore, they only wait until a special occasion to gift their spouse and most times that is a last-minute, half-baked plan. As mentioned, we are good at POP-UPs. Wayne will pop up in a heartbeat to bring me flowers, candy or a huge hug. We both love it. I love when I pop up on him. Today, I can say with a huge smile, my pop-ups are not to catch him doing wrong, but to catch him with a surprise look on his face.

The one time you pop-up, may be the one you're your spouse needs it most. You know what your spouse has to go through during the day, so encourage them. Don't let them wait until they get home to show them love. Pop up with a note on their tooth brush with a kind word, to get them through the day. Pop up in their lunch bag, with a picture of you. Pop-Ups need not be expensive. They just need to be often and genuine. Do a pop-up in his Bible with a photo of you. You can plan a pop-up with a love letter or poem in his suit coat or send him an email with a nice poem created by you or an inexpensive card with a message he needs to hear at that moment. Send him or her a sweet text message, which makes them anxious about coming home. They will look forward to what you have waiting for them. I love hiding little notes on Wayne's tooth brush. I have even popped up in his pajamas before he retired for bed. I slip a note in his pocket to let him know how he made my day.

Pop-Ups can be good, especially when you know what your spouse is facing outside the home. I love calling Wayne and when he asked, "What's up?" I reply "Nothing, I just wanted to hear your voice." I can hear his voice cheering up and before you know it, the conversation has catch Wayne doing wrong but to catch him to put a surprise look on his face. Now, we both are ready to get home in each other's arms.

I love when Wayne is watching one of those games he doesn't care about. I will sit with him for a while, until I know it's getting close to half time. I know he is just trying to wind down from the day. This is a good time for me to do a Pop-Up. He thinks I am gone to get ready for work the next day, until he sees I was planning my Pop-Up to be his half time show. I always remember, I am his half time show; otherwise, it will not be a good idea, if "Demboys or Cards" are playing, then the story will be a different story. So, make sure when planning a Pop-Up your timing is right.

But my husband loves planning Pop-Ups. He will Pop-Up by sending me flowers or by delivering them himself. His flowers never came without one of his beautiful poems. With originality he is good at that. Do what you're good at. I love when I go out to my car and he has placed a card in my seat or when he tells me to look outside my office window, telling me to come down so he can take me to lunch. There have been many times we met each other for lunch, to just sit and talk about us.

If your spouse is like mine, he doesn't like eating out much. He loves my cooking, but he loves taking me out for a break. I love dancing. So, I plan a Pop-Up, by cooking a real nice dinner for the two of us. This dinner may require us to both dress as if we were going to Jeff Ruby or Vincenzo. While I was planning dinner, Wayne was planning to take me for a dance. He knows I love to dance, especially as his private dancer. We dress up for the occasion. We spent no extra money, but the scenery and ambiance were set just right. All this was spontaneous. He knew we were going to dinner. However, he didn't know it would be at home. I knew he had plans to take me dancing, yet, I didn't know he had converted the living room into a Ballroom Dance Floor. We didn't have to leave our home, purchase gas, or wait around to be seated, etc… We enjoyed each other in the comfort of our own home. Due to our schedule, we do very little double dating. We stated back while planning our vacation that it would just be the two of us. We both look forward to this quality time together. We do go out and spend time fellowshipping with other couples, but it's not our typical date night. When we go on our dates, we want each other's undivided attention. Double dating causes one to give attention to someone other than their spouse. Sometimes you have to get rid of the thought of having to plan things out and just do a Pop-Up when that good thought comes to mind, even if it's at the last minute. Wayne is not a dancer, but within the confined walls of our home, he can cut a carpet. We both love when we can enjoy one another's company, have good clean fun and great fellowship after a great meal. Plus, it saves us money and grants us more time with each other. A couple should not have to spend money or leave their home to date and enjoy one another. We receive the same if not better results, as if we would have left our home. We both enjoys Pop-Ups. We are both able to satisfy the other one and ourselves by doing what the other person loves. Pop-Ups are not for the one performing it, though they can enjoy it. They are planned with the other person in mind to satisfy them.

Having a marriage with a goal to last forever, you must not focus on the negative things that went wrong or the mole hills. Often, we give too much energy and effort to the small things which prevents them from celebrating the awesome things they have accomplished in their marriage, especially during the terrible times.

MARRIAGE EVALUATION

1. Are we lacking in this area?

   _____

   _____

   If so, why?

   _____

   _____

2. Does one express their boredom in the relationship and need to do something different?

   _____

   _____

3. What can I do to improve in this particular area?

   _____

   _____

4. When you are your spouse go on dates, do you always invite other couples?

   _____

   _____

   _____

5. If so, would you be comfortable with just your spouse on a date?

   _____

   _____

If so, why?

_____
_____

6. What can my spouse do to improve in this particular area?

_____
_____

7. More examples?

_____
_____

8. How can I improve in this area?

_____
_____

When was the last time you were spontaneous?

_____
_____

Why?

_____
_____

When will we start planning Pop-Ups? *(Plan of Action)*

_____
_____

_____
_____
_____

What is hindering POP-UP in your marriage? *(Date of Completion)*

_____
_____

What can you do more of to spice up your spouse's day? *(Date of Completion)*

_____
_____
_____
_____

HONEY, I NEED YOUR SUPPORT NOT COMPLAINTS

When my husband was called into ministry over thirty years ago. It was very early in our marriage, when I was very immature. I complained about everything he did, everyone he met with, how much time I was not receiving. I wonder why we had to always go to church or do something related to church. If God told my husband to start a Spouse Nagging Ministry, I would have been the right person to lead that ministry. I feel embarrassed to say, "I was not supportive at all." I didn't like people, because it always seems to be some form of drama. I was very comfortable and satisfied with my small and selected circle. My mentality was if you made it to be part of my circle, you were blessed. I didn't like not going out clubbing, even though this was something I didn't do. I just knew our lifestyle was changing. I loved fixing my guest a Margarita on the house. I didn't mind going to church. I just didn't want to be the church or live according to what came from the Bible or the Preachers mouth. I was a faithful Sunday School and Bible Study student. I loved singing in the choir and the other choristers. These things I was doing before my husband was being called into ministry. When the Lord called him to be a

Deacon, I loved it. I love the seeing and hearing him pray and stand before the church to give an offertory appeal. He was a great speaker and everyone loved him. Therefore, I was the proud one with the pleasure of going home with him.

Those who know me knew I was Deacon Colbert's wife. I was in love with the thought of being married to Mr. Colbert, now Deacon Colbert. Therefore, I wore the title "Deacon's Wife" like a badge of honor, but not for the right reason.

The time came when I saw Deacon Colbert, serving in ministry is when my mindset changed, not at church, but at home. I couldn't understand, why of all people, particularly beautiful single women were calling my husband to pick them up for church. The thought of him being the Van Driver never crossed my mind. I was only concerned with him and them. I took things personal and to another level. I thought the best person to talk to about how I was feeling was myself or someone in a similar situation. Lord, and behold I found that person. We began to feed each other. The more we talked to one another, the more fuel we added to our negativity.

One day, when we were sitting at the dinner table, Wayne was not as talkative or looked as happy as he normally would. I finally got it together long enough to ask the right question. "Honey, what's wrong? You look like something is bothering you."

His response was "We'll talk." Then I thought, oh, the children are sitting here.

My youngest son, Jermaine, said "He's tired, from working all night and Damon didn't take out the garbage."

Everyone at the table laughed. We needed that ice breaker. Jermaine, and our daughter J'Keeta are good at bringing laughter. As always, serious Damon and Brandi didn't find it humorous.

Later that evening, I asked Wayne again, "What's wrong?" His response was "Kim, I need your support. I already have so much going against me. If I don't have your support, it will be almost impossible for me to succeed. That statement opened my eyes to my behavior. I had to choose as to whether or not I would be a supportive wife or a nagging spouse. I knew that if I decided not to support him, it would not only hinder his outside ministry, but our marriage.

I apologized to God first and then I asked Wayne to forgive me. Times when we know we are wrong are the times we need to admit it and correct those wrongs. I can tell

Wayne felt my sincere apology. He then asked me to join him in ministry. Lord, has this been a blessing. I knew little about ministry, but he was a great and patient teacher. During this lesson, Wayne expressed his need for my help by asking me to join him and I committed to support him with all sincerity. This lesson was deeper than I expected.

My serving alongside my husband in ministry has deepened my trust, love, and support for all he did. Most of all it drew me closer to God. One question in a relationship can make a difference. "Honey, what's wrong." This one question has taught me to not ask something, if I didn't want the answer. I had no idea what his response would be, but I'm so glad he didn't ignore it or put it off until a later day.

There are many areas where a spouse should be supportive.

- In the homes. What you do at home has a way of showing up in public. What your children see at home has a way of being mimicked. So, if it will not build up the family, ask yourself, "Should I do or say it."

- In building the trust fund. Regardless, if your spouse is working with the opposite spouse, don't trust the other person, but always trust your spouse. When the evil one tries to tell you otherwise, time to rebuke that devil.

Wayne and I, have vowed to allow no one to bring us negative information about the other one, which includes our parents. It is because we have established this commitment to God and one another, we can both declare by the Grace of God, no one has ever tried. We have learned that after we said our marital vow, we needed to continue making vows to one another. This has worked for over thirty years.

- In their Business Careers.

- In their Educational Careers.

- In their Church Ministries. Remember, your position. God, Spouse, and Church. Sometimes you may have to do it all, depending on your ministry. Then ask yourself, do I have to be the one who volunteers for everything. It is a great thing to serve in ministry, just remember, your marriage is a ministry and it should be your first and priority ministry.

- In parenting with children are from a previous relationship.

- In public. The worst thing a spouse can do is disrespect their spouse in public. Learn to wear your PDA, even if you let the house upset. No one needs to know you are having problems.

- In character, by refraining from anything with the opportunity to bring a bad reproach on you or your spouse.

- In financial support. If you know there is a financial crisis in the household, do what you can to support your spouse for bettering it, which means you may have to cook more and dine out less. If your husband falls on bad times, gets laid off, becomes ill, etc.… whereby he cannot provide financially as he did when you first become one, remember, this is not the time to point it out. It's time to help him, get to the place where he once was.

MARRIAGE EVALUATION

1. Does my spouse help me in the times of stress? If not why?

   _____
   _____

2. I wish my spouse would take more responsibility around the house? If not why?

   _____
   _____

3. Do I feel valued by my spouse? If not why?_____

   _____
   _____

4. Does my spouse support my emotional needs? If not why?

   _____
   _____

5. Does my spouse make me feel attractive? If not why?

   _____
   _____

6. Do I feel my spouse supports my ministry? If not why?

   _____
   _____

7. My spouse and I set aside time to talk about what is going on in our lives. If not why?

   _____
   _____

8. Do we spend time talking about the care of our marriage? If not why?

   _____
   _____
   _____

9. Do I feel comfortable telling my spouse, what I need? If not why?

   _____
   _____

10. My spouse and I have spiritual differences we cannot resolve. If not why?

    _____
    _____

11. What are some ways, my spouse can better support me? If no why?

_____
_____
_____

12. What are some ways my spouse hurts me? If not why?

_____
_____
_____
_____

www.ingramcontent.com/pod-product-compliance
Lightning Source LLC
Chambersburg PA
CBHW071215160426
43196CB00012B/2317